David Whyte's *Consolations* use everyday words to present us with a prism through which to better understand ourselves and the lives we walk through. At the request of readers globally, Whyte returns with fifty-two short, elegant meditations on a single word ranging from 'Anxiety' to 'Body', 'Freedom', 'Shame' and 'Moon'. He embraces their nuances, amplitudes and depths, and, in doing so, confronts realities that many of us would spend a lifetime trying to avoid.

In *Consolations II,* anxiety might be more mercifully understood as the preparation for being hurt, fixed beliefs are recognised as the very places where we do not wish to understand, guilt is a friend compassionately waiting for us to catch up and routine becomes a form of ritual and worship. Each piece in this life-affirming book is an invitation to slow down, shift our perspective and find comfort. In these pages, Whyte explores the full constellation of human experience.

CONSOLATIONS II

BOOKS BY DAVID WHYTE

POETRY

Songs for Coming Home
Where Many Rivers Meet
Fire in the Earth
The House of Belonging
Everything is Waiting for You
River Flow: New and Selected Poems
Pilgrim
The Sea in You
The Bell and the Blackbird
David Whyte: Essentials
Still Possible
The Seven Streams: An Irish Cycle

PROSE

The Heart Aroused:
Poetry and the Preservation of the Soul
in Corporate America

Crossing the Unknown Sea:
Work as a Pilgrimage of Identity

The Three Marriages:
Reimagining Work, Self and Relationship

Consolations:
The Solace, Nourishment and
Underlying Meaning
of Everyday Words

CONSOLATIONS II

The SOLACE, NOURISHMENT *and* UNDERLYING MEANING *of* EVERYDAY WORDS

DAVID WHYTE

MANY RIVERS PRESS

LANGLEY, WASHINGTON

www.davidwhyte.com

First published in the United States in 2025
by Many Rivers Press, P.O. Box 868, Langley, WA 98260

www.davidwhyte.com

A catalogue record for this book is available from
the Library of Congress.

ISBN 978-1-932887-59-4

Printed in the United States of America

Dedicated to

MICHEL DE MONTAIGNE

MY DISTANT, UNWITTING AND

ALWAYS MERCIFUL FRIEND

Our life consists partly in madness,
partly in wisdom. Whoever writes about it
merely respectfully and by rule leaves
more than half of it behind.

CONTENTS

CONTENTS *(continued)*

CONTENTS *(continued)*

ANGUISH

is the emblem of our helpless love, felt fully in every cell of the body; felt fully until it overflows, in a cry, in tears in words that try to negate, powerlessly, what is occurring. Anguish is our foundational cry against the unjust taking away of what we feel should be forever ours.

Anguish is a word that is a cry in itself: carrying the sound of the body feeling at last what it has all along needed to feel: a physical pain running right through our core and turned by the voice into the sound of pain itself, a pain we often previously could not imagine, an agony that is accompanied by the shock of absolute helplessness, a helplessness which is perhaps the very hallmark of human vulnerability itself, and that separates it from all the other manifold pains in a human life we have words to describe. Anguish is a force that racks and inhabits a suddenly surprised and now fully vulnerable, mind and body. But anguish fully felt is also the first stop on the road to recovery and healing.

Helplessness and the pains of helplessness are abiding companions to the experience of being human: the nurse by the dying child's bedside, having exhausted all remedies; the parent witnessing a teenager's first heartbreak, all of us in this world today, scrolling through the news, seeing the bombed-out homes of innocent, everyday people. We are made to experience both love and loss at an extraordinarily deep, bodily, everyday level and it may be that without helplessness we cannot experience love or loss fully and properly: anguish is the last fully felt measure of our care.

Feeling real, helpless, emotional pain, is also an entrance into the fully real and the fully felt and is an annunciation that we are actually paying attention at last - both to what is affecting us and the depth to which we are so movingly affected - anguish means we have finally felt and fully understood not only the true depth and foundational nature of our own suffering but the heartbreak that lies in every other human life we have ever touched or accompanied. Anguish is the doorway through which our personal suffering meets all the griefs that are shared by the world.

Anguish is only entered fully through the doorway of powerlessness and the absolute physical sense of helplessness. Anguish cannot be simulated: it is not only a measure of our care for others but the inability to know how or when or if it is possible to help, anguish is the very physical incarnation of our sense of compassion brought to ground at last, in the suffering body of the world - and in real anguish our body reciprocates - refusing to eat, losing weight, sitting alone, refusing to go out the door, full of the tremors and vulnerabilities that have accompanied human beings since the beginning of conscious time, vulnerabilities that at times, seem to arise from nowhere.

Anguish tells us that our deep sense of care has entered the timeless and the untouchable, that we have, for the moment, given up on solutions; stopped offering easy answers and let go of our previous, false sureties - anguish tells us we have finally decided to enter fully into the pain of our loss, or the pain of another.

The helpless pain at the centre of grief is the soul's annunciation that we might have arrived at suffering's essential core, where there is no ready way forward, no remedy for our suffering selves, no cure for a suffering loved one, or it seems, anything to be done about our distraught world.

Anguish is always waiting for us: beyond our refusing to care, or our unwillingness to feel fully how helpless we often are to help another, either those intimate to our lives or those suffering at a distance. Anguish is one of the most difficult qualities for human beings to enter because it is meant to be felt whether we have answers or not.

Anguish has its own sense of timing in both concentrating and inviting us to experience its pain, at what feels like a cellular level and then, soberingly, anguish stays longer than we would want and seems to have its own incredibly slow way of moving on. It seems not to move on in fact, until we have fully imbibed its painful instruction of how much we feel and how much we care.

Anguish is the act of finally allowing the transforming fire of care in the heart to rage fully at last, our defences burnt away by the consuming flame of our helpless love, where, at the centre of that fire, we feel our grief and loss to its very core and where grief, in its own timeless, unfathomable way, is allowed to slowly become its own cure.

Anguish fully felt and fully articulated in its helplessness, becomes in that articulation, the threshold where our private incurable, unspoken grief turns to public, passionate remedy. Anguish is the true, hidden, *a priori* foundation to our speaking out for others in this world, even those who seem to have hurt us, anguish is the only true ground we can stand upon to do any useful, charitable, philanthropic work.

Anguish is not debilitation: anguish fully felt, is a sign that we are fully awake at last, through our own pain, to all the heartbreaking losses and goodbyes involved in the drama of a human life, anguish tells us we are getting ready to embrace, or are even now, against our will, willing to embrace, what until now could never be embraced, that is: our ability to live fully in this body despite its never ending griefs and wounds, as others live, and have always lived, half helplessly, half trying to help, in the greater body of the suffering world.

ANXIETY

is the mask that truth wears when we refuse to stop and uncover its face. Anxiety is the disembodied state I feel when I pretend to put things right by worrying about them instead of truly conversing with them. Anxiety is the temporary helper going by the name of worry, who, when turned into our constant live-in companion, becomes our formidable jailor.

Anxiety means we haunt the body like an unhappy ghost from the past instead of living in it as a live anticipation of our future: anxiety creates the ghost-like sense of living timidly in our mortal frames so that we begin living in the world in the same way: as a troubled guest; a guest who does not believe they deserve the rest and hospitality that the body or the world can offer. Anxiety is the mind refusing to be consoled and nourished either by the body itself, or the world this body inhabits: anxiety is an extended state of denial; the refusal to put right something that needs to be put right, because putting it right means feeling real anguish, a real sense of the unknown and the need to change at a fundamental level.

Anxiety always tells us we are somehow just about to be injured by reality, by another or by the body itself: that nothing is to be trusted fully: our continued nervousness wasting the body's powers by keeping up a heightened but unsustainable level of alertness. Anxiety is difficult to shed because anxiety always refuses rest and rest is where the answer to anxiety lies. Rest feels as if we are letting down our guard and refusing to defend what we instinctively feel must be constantly defended to the last.

Temporary worry is useful to us and allows us to identify and innumerate what has not yet been fully answered or done and therefore outlines what is important to us and what we care about: constant worry always goes over and over the same territory and becomes, in the refusal to move on, the anxiety that cripples: anxiety is the illusory state of non-attention where we imagine that the very worrying itself is a way of paying deeper attention. Anxiety actually becomes our unconscious way of refusing to go any deeper with the things we are worrying about.

Constant anxiety is an unconscious defence against what is calling us to a deeper understanding. Ever-present anxiety actually covers over and prevents me from feeling fully what

I am worrying about. Constant anxiety is our constant way of not paying attention. Anxiety is the trembling surface identity that finds the full measure of our anguish too painful to bear, constant anxiety is our way of turning away from and attempting to make a life free from the necessities of heartbreak. Anxiety is our greatest defence against the vulnerabilities of intimacy and a real understanding of others. Allowing our hearts to actually break might be the first step in freeing ourselves from anxiety.

Anxiety is a way of being temporarily absent that almost always turns into a permanent exile. The exile that anxiety creates is most grievously felt in the way we both live in our bodies and don't live in our bodies at the same time. In order not to feel the full measure of my heartbreak, I refuse to let my body breathe in its own, easy natural way, I refuse to let myself feel I am in the right place at the right time; I refuse almost every invitational aspect of the world and see it only through the inverted telescope of my worries, where everything is made smaller, harder to see and harder to understand. My defence against a painful reality is to live in an unreal body in an unreal, besieged kind of time, and often in an unreal place I don't care about; I disallow myself the ability to stop and rest and the spacious silence needed for a full, easy, coming to ground in a new understanding.

In an anxious state I actually do not wish to understand, I only wish to worry: and in my worries, everything feels as if it is squeezed through the narrow aperture of my anxious body, causing it to tremble, to constrict and to hide inside that rheumatic constriction. I hurry from one thing to another, never actually landing, never feeling there is enough time, never making time to feel fully what is occurring both inside and outside my body. Anxiety, when I am lost, is often the only merciful way I can find to turn away from the pain the world caused me, is causing me and will cause me.

Anxiety is both my protection and the sure indication of my deepest vulnerabilities, all at the same time. What seems completely wrong with my life, with the world and with the time in which I live, is often my greatest, manufactured, defence against being fully part of this body, this world and this time. What I worry about and fret about for my children's future is often what keeps me from helping them into that future. What I worry about and what I am anxious about keeps me in an insulated, busy state of mind that stops me feeling the true depth and vulnerability of how much I care, how much I want to make a difference and how much I feel powerless to do it. Anxiety is my temporary ally and my daily saviour from the abiding pain of real heartbreak. I am not anxious because I worry so much as I am anxious because I do not want to feel the full vulnerability of being visible and touchable in a difficult world.

Our anxiety is constantly calibrated by the sense of being in the wrong place at the wrong time, inhabiting one moment while thinking about another, thinking one thing while doing another, trying to live in another abstracted, ideal body while forgetting to eat or breathe in this one. Loss of weight and loss of the breath are two abiding symptoms of anxiety. Gaining weight and breathing in a laboured way are also magnified by the abstractions of anxiety. Anxiety is my way of not fully feeling the vulnerability of my body, and my world.

Anxiety is my refuge but also, often the source of my loneliness doubling as it does as a defence by keeping people at a distance. Anxiety begins in helpless worry, and then becomes a means of protection against our own ability to help others, a state which provides me with distance from my real, foundational sorrow, by keeping an equal distance from the grief of others. I worry but other people's worries do not count.

Anxiety is a way of feeling constantly besieged and therefore allows me to be helpless to do anything about what lies beyond my walls. When I see everything as impinging on my life I find it hard to have a sense of humour about the fundamentally amusing absurdities of every human life; when I see everything as an ecological threat, I find it difficult to live with the blessings of birdsong or the beauties of a passing cloud scape. Anxiety is my ongoing excuse for not being intimate, anxiety is how I keep what I am worrying about from coming too close, anxiety enables me to stay well clear of my heartache.

Over time, constant anxiety is a form of amnesia, a forgetting and an absence. Anxiety becomes my beloved abstraction where I can keep myself in suspension, when I am afraid of getting to the bottom of things and allowing myself a true understanding. Emotional immobility is the state in which we find ourselves when we have lost sight of the silent, pivotal centre from which to speak, to take action or to harvest the wisdom of the spacious, the timely and the timeless.

Anxiety is produced by a dynamic of the mind whose chief evolutionary task is actually to make us more anxious: to worry, to fret, and out of that worry and fret, to get things done, and out of getting things done, to survive; constant anxiety always in the end raises even the tiniest little threat to the level of existential survival. Anxiety makes every little thing a matter of life and death.

The cure for anxiety is almost always found in some kind of radical simplification, a simplification that slowly opens up a very physical, rested experience of timelessness. Often the heart of our simplification is the freeing realisation that we can do nothing about the worry except to let it go. From this place we learn not to leave our worries behind but to consciously worry only for brief necessary periods when worry is needed as a way of paying deeper attention. To briefly, consciously, worry in a way that brings things to a proper harvest of presence is always far more helpful than days of vague anxiety.

One of the greatest gifts we can give to our friends, our partners, our children or our colleagues, might be to forsake anxiety: to realise how much we use our worrying as a barrier to our becoming and a protection against real intimacy, real friendship and real engagement with our work. One of our greatest gifts as a provider might be to stop all the worrying about those we are providing for; to provide something else, something that is more difficult to give but something they might actually want - a deeper more rested, and invitational sense of presence and the gift of timelessness in that presence.

Luckily, all of our great contemplative traditions tell us that the way out of anxiety is always very close, and abides just beneath the very surface of our worries, waiting for us to drop down into the body again to a better place. Every meditational tradition of mindfulness in the world tells us that our doorway to freedom is as simple and as close as learning to take the next breath, to take that breath as fully as possible, and then to learn how to give it easily back into the world. In breath and out breath, when taken and when given and when completed without a controlling, worrying thought is an instant doorway to release from anxiety. A mindful easing away from the restless, bullying, fretful mind, into the restful, invitational calmness of easy breathing is always the foundation from which we will re-inhabit the mind in a more spacious, generous, less worrisome way.

Anxiety and all the ways we feel the tremulous symptoms of anxiety tell us just how far away we are from inhabiting a real sense of the timeless. Anxiety is not an answer to a problem we are worrying about but the measure of our distance from the place where the answer lies. Our ability to escape from anxiety is found in our ability to do the simplest thing and to do it well: to breathe and to live easily in our breathing. This truth is too simple for the anxious mind to believe, therefore it is best to breath in silence first and tell ourselves that we'll get to curing our anxiety later. Anxiety cannot cure itself, the cure arrives while we are giving ourselves a real sense of rest. Anxiety is often created by trying to remember everything and keep it straight in our harried minds. No wonder then, that the cure for anxiety is found in learning to forget the self that first felt the fateful need to worry.

BACKGROUND

is not the shy, retiring, you-go-first word it seems to want to be. Background is underestimated and calls on us to widen our vision and open to a greater breadth of attention.

Foreground dominates our lives, is overestimated in importance and hides the greater context from which it has emerged. The neglect of background is the source of much of our present loneliness and most definitely, our present unhappiness.

Background is always what we start to pay attention to when we start to pay real attention. In Zen practice, one of the signs of deepening states of presence and intimacy with our surrounding reality is the way background stops being background: the way we stop choosing between near and far, past and present, near objects and those that seem to lie over the horizon of our understanding. Background shapes our seeing of a thing as much as the thing itself: the sun around a silhouetted maple actually outlines what we see as the shape of the tree. A tree in our real, grounded, physical apprehension of the world is made of light and its absence, as much as it is made of wood.

Foreground has come to be a kind of obsession in our lives making us unwitting slaves to too many of the things that are placed right in front of our noses: numbers, results, graphs, the blurred screen full of endless messages. We obsess with what individual people seem to be saying to us rather than the vaster sweep of human mythological dynamics that lie behind their speech. Facebook under all its multi-headed disguises of Instagram, WhatsApp and Threads is aptly named: trying as it is to be the first thing we see, everyday, in front of our noses, literally in our faces.

Foreground is where we recognise too late, in the news, most of our problems but also, most of the possibilities that have just slipped through our hands, all of which can only emerge from the greater context behind the news: the living, breathing ever evolving background. Foreground, without background is where we always come to recognise things too late. The ability to pay attention to background from the very beginning grants us a disguised clairvoyance in making it look as if we are able to look into the future. We understand what is about to happen, by looking now at the background, from where all our problems and possibilities first emerge.

Paying attention to background as much as foreground is not only an introduction to our greater surroundings: paying attention to background tells us we are already in a conversation with greater worlds and have been for longer than we know. Bringing background into our life tells us how much we have been defending and fighting against acknowledging everything that has been there all along and has often been travelling faithfully from afar to knock on our door.

Background and backdrop is the ultimate context of community. The birdsong, the wind in the trees, the eyes of the passing stranger trying to catch our eye for a morning hello; and even, and at the end of our walk, the warm hubbub of a coffee shop filled with waking voices. Background is our substrate of belonging, a shared communal background is our first remedy for loneliness.

We have grown and evolved over the millennia with the green of grass and leaves to find every shade of that colour soothing and inviting, and with the wind ruffling the blades, to find refreshment: with the blue of the sky to find it scintillating, and with the spaciousness it creates in our minds, literally up-lifting. We are lonely today, not because we are losing contact with other individuals, but because we have lost our friendship with the sky and the moon and the stars that create the canopy beneath which all of our human relationships and friendships flourish and prosper in mutual awe.

Direct contact with another foreground face and constant contact with all the foreground explanations we conspire to make together, is only a temporary cure for loneliness, often leading to disappointment in the specifics of a too predictable story and a too familiar life. To share the breezy morning sky by the broad Atlantic with a passing stranger or live music when crammed into a pub full of unknown but foot-tapping fellow listeners is another form of closeness, one sustained by a friendship with the wider world rather than making foreground relationships and foreground naming bear all the weight. Background is strangely a doorway to a close up intimacy, one that does not need the burden of asking of the relationship - 'What now?'

We share a sky, the sound of the rain, the appreciation of music with almost all our fellow human beings. The shared, greater context of our surrounding life is what grants the real possibility of deep friendship to our foreground friends. Even prisoners who rarely see the sky but who share a proper sympathetic understanding of their enclosed background, and their curtailed background lives, are given, through their prison walls, the possible intimacies of friendship.

Background is half of what we see and hear; background is half of what we do not see and hear. Background is our visible and invisible helpmate, waiting for us to raise our heads to look and see. Background is the constellation of swirling forces out of which our life emerges, and background holds our future, the horizon in our life that always draws us on; a life that can find true definition only through what always lies beyond it.

BELIEFS

are not sacred, only the places and experiences from which they arise are sacred. What we call a belief is often only the superstructure that is left when the original, physical, transformative understanding has retreated to the rear of our experience and now needs to be explained in personal recall or in a communal, after-the-fact, reassurance. Beliefs that we need others to share are most often representations of our secret disbelief in what was once a palpable living presence, which is why our beliefs are held so passionately, and so ruthlessly: defending as we do, most vociferously, what we are already in the process of losing. The only real invitation to belief, and to believe in what I believe, is through my actions: actions that tell others that I still actually remember.

Beliefs, most particularly the beliefs that must be believed by others, are the measure of my disbelief in what I originally experienced: which is why the passionate beliefs of others are almost always too tedious to bear, except unfortunately, by the person who holds them. Beliefs invite disbelief. Even people who generally agree with one another are almost always irritated by the minor differences of interpretation they unfailingly discover on further conversation. My belief is never exactly your belief, and from a practical point of view, my belief can never be exactly your belief: belief is about fixing the world in place; no human being ever fixes the world in place in exactly the way their neighbour does. Therefore, in a never ceasing, moveable world, fixed beliefs are the beginning of all unhappiness between human beings.

The part of the human mind that holds a fixed belief is the part of the mind that from an evolutionary point of view needs to name things and name them exactly, even if the name is not true, to create a common language within a community or in order to grant us an illusory sense of control in a constantly moving, restless world. The naming mind does not like to live with ambiguity, and yet the world is constantly creating ambiguity as to our next move. The naming mind thinks we are jeopardising our sense of survival by not believing one thing over another or one thing or another - the naming mind is right: beliefs are about survival, and shared beliefs about communal survival, not about really understanding anything to the core or the truth behind the belief itself. Shared beliefs are temporary truces between argumentative human beings. Beliefs are generally not to be believed, and disturbingly, not even my lack of belief in belief should be accepted.

The part of my mind that carries a fixed belief is the part of me that cannot countenance another parallel or equally true belief. Criminal science tells us that our abilities to report or remember accurately what we witness is extremely low: just as low is our ability to witness reality in general without mistaking what we see or hear - most definitely in these days, in what we absorb and then pass on through the internet. The profusion of conspiracy theories at present represents our out of control necessity to believe even the strangest beliefs and then join with a mass of others in that delusion. We live in a time where even a tiny eccentric minority of the planet can make the strangest belief, a mass delusion and a mass movement, held by millions.

No matter how fantastic or even deeply felt our beliefs may be, fixed beliefs have to be defended and supported, and per force, in a very moveable, changeable world, by false or manufactured evidence. Other people's beliefs hold a strange combination of being incredibly boring and incredibly deadly at one and the same time. Beliefs held privately may be given the sanctity of self-examination to see how or how not they might be true as we test them on the world. Beliefs held publicly, held in place and defended, are always predictable in their ability to divide the believer from the non-believer.

Beliefs are a constant invitation to disbelief at the distance they create, between the one who thinks their life depends upon their belief, and the one who doesn't think that particular belief even worth taking the time to think about; between the one who is at the centre of the power structure the belief has created, and that other, historically long-suffering person, the one who is just going along, in fear of their social lives or their actual lives, pretending to believe in order to survive. Beliefs stand at the crossroads of both individual human revelation and communal confusions when knowledge is warped by power: life-giving in their original emergence, astonishingly boring and controlling in the details and in the rules they need others to go along with and deadly in their coercion of a world that does not comply.

Beliefs are magnificent stories immobilised to narrow interpretations and then harnessed for a whole spectrum of human needs, but always in the end, when taken literally, as a way to garner power over others. Beliefs taken on by groups or societies always complicate and cover over the original spirit that originated the belief in order to preserve the power of those who now reserve for themselves the sole right to interpret the belief itself: the simple teachings of Jesus rendered into astonishingly grotesque, power-mad statues of medieval Popes bursting out of the walls of the Vatican, the same, simple teachings of love transformed into the political hatreds that characterise modern American right-wing evangelism, and for the American left: fine, original, sensitivities to race and gender, become mono-maniacal concerns to the exclusion of any other subject: again in Islam, the fresh, early revelations issuing from the silence and quiet drip of stalactites in a cool cave in the deserts of Arabia, now used by older men to manipulate younger, inexperienced men into suicide.

There is nothing wrong with beliefs held privately, except our belief that it is necessary for other people to share the same beliefs with me. No matter what innate goodness was in my original belief it is always, when carried too far, superseded by my belief that others who do not agree with this goodness should come to a very bad end.

Beliefs are deeply personal, felt in a very inchoate, physical way, experienced over time in differing forms of seasonality and harvested differently throughout an individual growing life or the growing life of a community: they are almost impossible to translate specifically to another person's understanding - except through art, through poetry, through inspirational story, in other words, through a real, invitational conversation where the arrived understanding is always in doubt, always temporary and mutually nourishing.

Belief stops being merely belief and becomes real presence when the unknown is kept alive, where what is living in my belief is kept alive by the way I keep testing that belief in the real world and in the unknown world that awaits me.

Shared beliefs, bereft of the unknown, or the arts that bring us into contact with the unknown, almost always involve a great deal of shared pretence: pretence that we are all talking about the same thing, that my imagination or even experience of the divine corresponds exactly with yours: the illusion that when I speak to God and you speak to God, or you over there, refuse to speak to God, we are all strangely, talking about the same God. To contradict us all, most probably and thankfully it is almost certain that God stands beyond all belief.

One particular dynamic that has always been particularly hard to believe is that human beings have always believed incredibly unbelievable, hard-to-believe things and then gone about using those fictions to make other people's life a misery.

Once momentum is behind a certain belief, whole industries of thought align behind it to create salaries and livings out of persuading other people that the unbelievable and the not to be believed is believable and everyday. One of the refreshing if difficult dynamics of our times is the rightful, instinctual refusal to automatically take on inherited beliefs.

The astonishing but disturbing truth, is that what I believe in, is probably the least interesting thing about me. What I believe in, entirely and separately from you is not a real conversation with anything other than what I wish to be true. If I want to bore the world in general, let me tell everyone my tedious, boring, eccentric, always, slightly unbelievable set of beliefs. Beliefs, as opposed to a living conversation with what invites me in and draws me on, always sap enormous energy from a human life. My belief needs constant reinforcement, constant maintenance and constant coercion of others in order for me to continue in my enclosed and endorsed understanding.

Fixed beliefs have consequences in a human life: where reality does not align with my belief, I have to stop paying attention and turn my face away, I have to actually absent myself from reality in order to continue thinking the world is made exactly the way I and my co-believers have been telling ourselves it has always been made.

Finding belief in others uninteresting does not mean that we turn away from the person themselves, or the living wellsprings of the story from which the beliefs have come: they are in fact an invitation to understand why this person thinks it so necessary to have these strange, unaccountable, fixed beliefs. Finding specific beliefs about as interesting as watching paint dry does not mean we turn away from the great mythological and psychological explorations that run through the stories of every religion and every inheritance. Belief always becomes more real and more interesting through the way I live my life in its presence and in the witness of my unfolding understanding.

Mercy can be a meritorious abstract belief, and mercy can also be useless to believe in if we do not actually learn to care for others, and care for others' lives, if we do not live mercy consciously and unconsciously in every cell of our very human body and in every coming together in human community. Mercy and care are questions always being asked and always asking to be answered. My belief in mercy probably has nothing to do with understanding true mercy, most especially in the way I am merciless with those who do not agree with my specific ways of believing in mercy. The Resurrection is not just a belief: but a felt experience that occurs again and again in a human life as we bring ourselves back from the dead in every succeeding loss and disappearance. The Resurrection is not just for people who believe they are Christians: resurrection belongs to everyone.

The human mind is both wondrous and exceedingly eccentric and strange, all at the same time. When confronted with dynamics the mind cannot resolve, it will attribute temporary names to the un-understandable, and then start to shape its identity around those temporary descriptions. What was meant to be the beginning of a conversation becomes a belief that ends the conversation.

Belief is often my act of defence and preservation: belief keeps a part of me alive that I know will disappear if I have a real conversation with the unknown. Beliefs must be defended, beliefs are the foundation of all dead-end arguments.

Beliefs are held by only a very small part of the mind: even true believers have large parts of their psyches that do not participate or believe in their beliefs. Hence the abiding red thread of hypocritical sinfulness that has always run so satisfyingly through every self-satisfied religion on earth. Belief is only what I have chosen to believe, out of an enormous conversational constellation of qualities and understandings that reside like a living ecology in my being.

Holding to a belief through thick and thin is often associated with courage: human beings will go to the stake over the tiniest shade of interpretation, but perhaps it takes an even greater courage to live in conversation with the great unknown that is constantly pulling us by the collar, up and over the horizon of our ability to name and categorise. To live fully, in the constant gravitational field of arriving 'beautiful questions', without fixing them into beliefs, is to become fully incarnated and fully here: to live without barriers and beliefs is to ask the beautiful, invitational question: and to become an invitation ourselves: seeing others and their approach to life as an intriguing, surprising conversation always worth having.

It is possible to live and to live well without fixed beliefs: borne along by the great flow of human experience, stories and mythologies out of which every fixed belief was wrought. Beliefs held by others are always a combination of the strange and, when repeated too much, the incredibly boring: but what lies behind the ancient human fixation on belief is the life blood and the endless drama of our human inheritance and the beating, questioning heart of every individual life who wishes to know what they might be involved with in this existence.

Living without fixed beliefs strips me down to a radical sense of simplicity, and a radical sense of presence, to the foundational, simplifying, invitational question itself: what if I could love the world just as it is and what if I could love everyone and every last thing in it, just as they are: untouched, untrammelled and completely innocent of my own, strange, coercive inherited, or invented way of seeing the world? Perhaps the healthiest belief of all, is one that disarms all the rest: the belief that fixed beliefs are the enemy of all human peace, personal and public. Through that belief we allow every belief, most especially my own, to be more of a curious invitation, a way to come to an understanding, a beautiful question leading all of us together, to somewhere better, beyond belief. As one famous Zen master said to his temporarily lost student: 'Not knowing is most intimate.'

BLESSING

is not just the act of wishing something good for someone else: the art of blessing is the act of wishing something for someone that they had not allowed themselves to desire or deserve. Someone with the power to bless is someone who recognises what is hidden in another that they have not dared to articulate themselves. Blessing is sudden permission to desire what we have desired at a foundational level all along.

In a true blessing what was hidden is made visible, what could not be said is said, even if it is by another witnessing presence. Blessing is the art of bringing things alive so that they can be felt and experienced in their true essential form. To bless the day, as they say in Ireland, is to anticipate some surprise about to be made known to us, out of the wild blue yonder of the hours to come. Blessing is an act of refusing to take the day or the ordinary for granted: a way of calling out the extraordinary from the ordinary: the blessing of the morning light, the blessing in a good welcome, the blessing of having slept well, the blessing in our child's face. What is seen to be looking back at us through the act of blessing calls out something from deep inside us that we did not fully know was there, until we blessed it. Blessing is a form of paying exquisite attention to what we are trying to bless. Blessing deepens our attention.

Blessing is a way of making an invitation to what lies beneath the often dazzling, reflected, confusing surface of our lives. Blessing calls on what has waited for us all along and speeds its arrival. A true blessing is a way of readying the one who is blessed.

Blessings are always mercifully short; blessings bless us in the very act of moving on quickly once they have been said, leaving us alone and surprised into thinking: what might we be, or what might we want, or what we might give; that we had been, until now, and until the moment we were so blessed, too afraid to admit

BODY

might be a word that represents something more miraculous than even the mind that can contemplate the body's miraculousness. Perhaps the central and unchanging difficulty for human beings in remaining healthy, physically and psychologically, is that the mind cannot fully contemplate, appreciate or understand the body's thousands of interlocking inter-dependent connected systems, and the way those hidden systems connect with the world: the way the body's never ceasing, beating, pumping, circulating, breathing in and out busyness, all combined with its inner restful autonomic guidance, needs no act of will or effort or management on our part to keep it going. The mind unanchored in the body is always trying to be something or somebody, the mind is always attempting to control the body: the body exists in its own form of freedom, always under the gravitational influence of something far beyond the mind's understanding.

The body when healthy, makes the busy mind uncomfortable in its astonishing, rested complexity, asking for no immediate solution or help in its need to create another heartbeat or the next breath. The only part of the mind that can truly understand the body is the part of the mind that is, through silence and rest, able to be welcomed back fully into the body's equally rested and gifted sense of presence, creating as its culmination, the deep undergirding consciousness, and the marriage of real physical presence with a good thinking mind, a coming together that has always been revered in our ancient traditions.

The mind after all, only escapes its own false, manufactured reality, by seating itself in the unmediated reality of the body's seeing, hearing and sensing: the mind thus seeing through the body's eyes, learning through its ears, grieving through its wounds and through its extraordinary ability to touch and be touched.

The mind untethered from the body always tries to confuse the body in turn; tries to set it against itself: the abstracted mind, trying to protect itself, trying to compensate for its distance, asks simultaneously, for far too much and far too little from the body: the dislocated mind always asks it to eat too much, drink too much, worry and fret too much and then, at the same time, asks it not to feel too much, not to grieve too much, not to feel the wounds it has actually experienced, asking it in effect not to heal itself in ways that might undercut the surface life we have artificially manufactured through our distance.

No matter all this subterfuge to cover up the body's vulnerability: the mind is actually ashamed of its distrust in the body's willingness to be truthful in its experience and what it has experienced. Much of our outer forms of shame stem from this central sense of not measuring up to the very thing that houses all and any thoughts we might have on the matter. The fearful mind will not let the body move, not let the body dance, not let the body grieve or risk itself, as it was made to risk itself in the physical world and the vulnerable intimacies of that world.

The abstracted mind, separated from its absolute anchorage in time and space granted by the physical structure it was born into, does not know quite what to do with the body: which it would like to disown, with all its aches and pains, its wounds and its deeply honest memories of how and where those wounds were delivered.

The unanchored mind in its disbelieving of the miracle of the body, in its loss of faith in the portal that the body provides, in its lack of understanding of the way the body is constantly seeking its own psychological cures and remedies through both memory and anticipation and then through its heartfelt dedication. The disembodied mind is always trying to substitute another story for the body's actual story, always attempting to manufacture other events and other interpretations, for actual events and actual consequences.

The mind cannot quite believe the way that the body does not wish to be healed in ways that ignore, trample on or obscure its very own, hard earned, wounded experience of life. The unanchored mind wishes to live forever. The body knows it has already experienced an infinity of lifetimes by virtue of its essential vulnerability; the way it dies into each waiting passage of life: a vulnerability it shares with all other physical touchable bodies on this earth.

But seated in the body once again, through trauma, through grief, through the vulnerabilities of illness or the imminence of death: we find out just how much the body loves the mind when that mind has come back to live in the body: how much it has missed its intimate presence, how much it wants to invite it home again. A good death is always marked by the abstracted mind finding a welcome home again in the experience, the poignant physical memories and the vulnerabilities of the body, no matter how wounded the body might be, nor how wounded the mind that needs a home might be.

No matter how long the mind has been away, creating its own tortured world, the body always wants the errant mind back, always, like a good father or mother, is waiting at the door, always, always, always, ready with a welcome home.

BRAND

is not something an individual human being should want for themselves. Brand is meant to mark ownership or consistency and should be confined to what can be owned or forced into compliance. Brand is a false substitute for a truly moveable, unnameable, unquantifiable, living, growing identity. To be branded is to have a mark of ownership literally seared into our skin for all to see. Brand is an immoveable image that stays with us through every seasonality, something that cannot be erased, something that a human being shouldn't want, something that says I belong to someone else's imaginings and assessments and am therefore, always at the bidding of someone else: my boss, my audience, my following.

Branded means we are marked for life, marked to someone else's account: owned and corralled in order, and originally, in the instance of cattle, to be sent to an untimely end. Branding diminishes the elemental valency of human identity: where our valency is measured by our ability to combine and be available for the unrecognisable, the unnameable and the inconceivable. Branding may be appropriate for a can of well-loved beer, for a medical company who guarantees the safe production of their drugs, or for the representation of any collective effort, but for an individual human being, making a brand of themselves, is to be held and imprisoned by that brand. Branding is the death of both humanity and individual artistry.

All true artists refuse to comply with the language or behaviours of branding: all true artists shed their hides multiple times in their lives, letting any trace of a fixed mark fall away in the process. What is worth wearing for a while is always in the end worth discarding. We are what we wear, only while we wear it, what is worth wearing is always in the end worth giving away, back to the place it came from.

Brand is the mark on our surface skin, it cannot penetrate to the depth to which we wish the world to find us. Branding is my temporary surface name, my false home and my present protective disguise. Branding is what I give up doing in order to become real.

BREATH

is a word that wants us to live in our mouths in the same way that it can live in our own bodies: without undue effort, and left to itself, rely on the easy, rested, autonomic give and take of the body itself. Real rest is the breath simply looking after itself and looking after everything else as it does it. Breath is not only an invitation into the body but the essence of the way we already know how to live in that body. Easy, relaxed, breathing always leads to surprise: at how centred we already are, how unhurried we are underneath it all, how patient we never knew we could be.

Breath is a word that breathes deeply of its own self, asking us in turn to breathe even as we follow its long, stretching vowel sound and its gentle, arriving tide of air that in the end, forms the sweet final sound of the word itself, flowing out of our bodies and into the waiting, listening world. Breath is a self-compassionate word that is difficult to pronounce harshly. In speaking the word breath, the last soft ending in the very last letters are like the sound of water coming to rest on a sloping beach, telling us in affect of the way our breath has reached within the word itself some shoreline upon which it will rest and then recede and return again, back into the very body that was so instrumental in its first creation.

Breath is the very tidal word that carries the very essence of our very tidal identity, where just the act of saying the word, culminates in that momentary, invitational silence at its end, out of which the next in-breath is naturally born.

Physiologically we do not need to breath in, we just need to breathe out fully and the in-breath follows as natural as the body's natural wish to go on living. We are tidal creatures; always giving and always waiting to receive; always arriving and always about to say goodbye: we begin in some form of silence, live through the breathing exchange of a given life and end again in another form of silence. We are here and we are somehow not quite, a coming and a going, and in every religious inheritance, breath is the essence of that understanding, of our passing through, of our poignant transience, the way we appear and disappear. Breath is the essence of prayer.

Breath is the very first thing we give to this world and the very last thing we are allowed to take from it.

Breathing is what we do before we understand a single thing about our world, and the last thing we will do despite all of our hard-earned wisdom. The first breath an infant takes and the last breath they will take, an hour later or many years later are both seen intuitively, no matter our beliefs, no matter if we are religious or not, as moments of pure holiness, whether their life in between could be described that way or not. Breath bookends our life but also every single moment of our lives; between each breath is where everything happens, and where, if we really inhabit the breath everything that happens is magnified.

We arrive on the tide of the unspeakably profound and are carried away by that same current at the very end, but all along, and in our life in between, breath generously accompanies us through every day of our existence whether our lives are long or too short, happy or unhappy, successful or unsuccessful, healthy or not healthy - and breath never gives up until the body's final giving up - breath guides us even through sleep, through every second of our seemingly unconscious nights. Breath is the essence of generosity in its thankless companionship and the emblem of faithfulness in its constant visiting and its momentary merciful absences, fetching and carrying for us without our thanks or appreciation; inviting and reassuring, no matter our outward difficulties: breath is one of the few dynamics in our wilful lives that works constantly on our behalf without needing coercion, praise or even forceful encouragement. Breath invites us to live our life as generously and as easily in its giving and taking as breath itself.

Breath is the essence of aroma, our sense of smell mediated through the flow of the breath, breath is our intimate exchange between the inner and the outer, the perfume of roses, the robust presence of leather and horse flesh, the breath of another we experienced in a first kiss. Breath is an oceanic give and take that can make meeting into love making.

Breath is practical and helpful in understanding how we should be in life: the unquenchable source of both visible and invisible help in our days, giving when we do not ask, teaching us, with each in-breath, how to receive when we feel we do not deserve to receive. Breath is the invisible made visible, the intangible made touchable and real. In every in-breath we receive through intangible oxygen, the life blood of what to us, is an invisible world, to enliven and invigorate our heart, our limbs and our eyes - and in every out-breath we provide that other not-to-be-seen miracle nourishment of carbon dioxide, something every green leaf desires and needs, to turn a sapling into a full grown tree. Every breath we release in to the air gives life to almost every living green thing we can see, the structure of every plant and tree comes as much from the carbon in the air we breathe out as it does from the minerals they find through their roots.

Breath becomes our other human essence when we shape it into every day speech, or extraordinary song: we are virtuoso players of the breath, forming thousands of words, and tens of thousands of nuances in words, simply by passing the breath up through the throat, around the tongue and out of the shapes of an extraordinarily mobile mouth.

Through the breath and through the words formed by our breath we advertise the essence of our character, but also, all of our manifest flaws: our attempts at manipulation or coercion, our falsity and even our diseases are all manifest in the way the breath inhabits our words. As human beings, we listen unconsciously to another's breathing and the way that breath moves through their speech, in order to establish who we are with and how much, in effect, we should trust the being that is breathing through words in such intimate proximity.

We also listen longingly for the nobility of ease that can be carried so admirably by speech: for generosity, for the perfect pitch of giving and receiving that is emblematic of the best of human character: words fully imbued with the breath and with the presence and with the nourishing grain of truth. Breath calibrates the ease and generosity of our words, the way we grant life to words or rob them of meaning, the way we enliven or do not enliven others through the way we breathe and the way we speak. Short speech is literally created through short breathing. The steadiness and surety of the breath in speech is a measure of the steadiness and surety of our lives, and then, out of that, the surety of all the lives for which our speech makes us responsible.

Breath anchors and holds us practically in the rhythm of time and the rhythm in each and every moment of our days while holding within its amplitude and depths, the door to exalted states of bliss and presence. Breath is the alpha and omega of our being, the essence of our ability to give and to receive; breath sustains our everyday practical existence, while beckoning us into the the deeper timeless tidal rhythms beyond any possibility glimpsed in our every day life.

Breath is both the practical biological essence of life itself and an invitation to a life beyond the predetermined and the merely biological: a parable telling us how to live, how to give and receive, and how in the most restful way, to let it all go in the end. Every breath, fully taken, is our daily, unconscious, reconnaissance of the invisible frontier between life and that mysterious, literally breath-taking giving-up we have only arbitrarily decided to call a death.

BURNOUT

is a word that conjures a hollowed out, blackened centre, now lying, due to our exhaustion, not only at the very core of our body but of our way of being. Burnout feels like a living central absence, not only of a centre, but the sources that used to rise from that centre.

The exhaustion of burnout always recalls a previously felt internal fire, one from which our unquenchable energies once emerged. Burnout denotes a kind of amnesia: not only in the forgetting of our very personal priorities but the inability to locate a source inside us that previously seemed to run through all the seasons of our life. This loss of a fiery essential centre is also experienced as a loss of faith: a form of forgetting, not only that the source actually existed inside me in the first place but that I might not now ever remember how to drink from it again.

Burnout is diagnosed by exhaustion, often caused by calling on energies in work or family life, that are not native to my way of being: the necessity of having had to use my will to keep going hour after hour, day after day; of assuming goals that actually belong to other people and which I have stolen to my detriment.

Burnout always involves a loss of the timeless and therefore of the ability to rest. Burnout, in a very profound way, is a loss of friendship with time itself, a daily existence that can no longer honour the specific gifts and seasonality of the hours that guide me through the day. Exhausted, I no longer appreciate an early misted morning, a long slow afternoon or the preparations for an evening gathering. Everything is in the way of everything else, and everything is a barrier to my becoming; irritation becomes my constant companion. Burnout is the experience of feeling continually out of season: spring might as well be summer and summer might as well be autumn and could just as well be winter, everything becomes something to get through, but where everything also seems to be going straight through me, without touching the sides.

In the loss of faith in existence itself, we refuse, in a kind of symmetrical sympathy, to fully exist ourselves. Being out of season with the outside world means we also miss our own inner, creative, tidal comings and goings. Burnout's ultimate tragedy is that we cannot even recognise who or even what we are missing in our life: we stop recognising what possibilities are coming and going, who has entered and who has actually left. Burnout prevents me from loving, burnout is our inability and then our refusal to love the harvests and riches of time.

Burnout calls for creative breakdown, either in submitting to unconscious self-sabotage, the way that disasters large and small seem to track our exhausted burned-out self on a daily basis, the way we actually create those disasters unknowingly ourselves, trying to make a break for freedom or to create a conscious creative breakdown. Burnout is often as much the resistance to making these changes as being worn down by what we cannot seem to change: all the ways I find it impossible to leave the job, or leave the relationship; all the ways I find it impossible to change my approach to work, or all the ways I need to simply learn to love again must be looked at and allowed to break down and fall away: breaking down perhaps, the expensive life that holds me, day after day, a hostage to fortune. Burnout calls for stopping the conversation before it stops me entirely. Burnout calls for a courageous claiming, I need to recognise that I do need a holiday, a break, a pilgrimage away from the familiar - and for much longer than anyone else will allow me.

Burnout calls for self-love through the specifics of affectionate memory and the self-compassion in understanding why we were willing to give up so much in the first place. I trace my path to exhaustion through the very things I laid aside on the way here. The very path I took to arrive at this hollowed-out, burned-out state, is the path I will take out of my imprisonment, back to what is precious to me, back to a newly found energy and freedom. I look at each giving up in my memory and I see why I thought it would protect me or give me false respect in other's eyes. I take time to remember what I loved and have always loved since I was a child, I do not try to burden that love by forming plans around how I can create a job or a project around it, I simply try to remember and experience the love again. I bring that long lost love, inside or outside, into the present hours of my day again. I build my life again, slowly, step by step, around that source.

In our forgetting, burnout describes a loss of dreams. Burnout is a discarded friendship with what could be described as our inner dream body: the very physical place where our enthusiasms and willingness to travel far horizons were generated. Burnout is a loss of friendship with a very personal sense of the unknown: the unknown life that until now, has always drawn us on, and still wants to draw us on, beyond our present goals and daily concerns.

Burnout's deleterious effects are always magnified by the elimination of the very thing that might save us: the longing for something other than the very life that is now wearing us down. But burnout fully realised is also the decisive, exhausted moment in which we realise we cannot go on in the same way.

Not being able to go on, is always in the end, a creative act, the threshold moment of our transformation away from physical exhaustion. Not being able to go on is the beginning of a proper relationship with the timeless and the healing possibilities of timelessness: healing ourselves from burnout always involves a reacquaintance with the eternal: my ability to experience the timeless is a parallel to my ability to rest.

The foundation from which we transform the experience of burnout is always the realisation that we have been measuring all the wrong things in all the wrong ways and that we have for too long, mis-measured our sense of self in the same way; that we have allowed the shallow rewards of false goals or false people to mesmerise, bedazzle and entrain us: to hide from us an ancient and abiding human dynamic - that we belong to something greater and even better for us than the realm of the measured.

In trying to measure up in ways that do not fully have our measure, we make ourselves immeasurably smaller. The realisation and understanding that we are, after all, completely burned out is always sobering, always astonishing in how much it reveals the depth of our exhaustion, but it is also our first step toward reclaiming, not only our ability to rest in the timeless, but at the other side of not being able to go on, the invitation to a renewed and emboldening sense of a freedom reclaimed.

doesn't care that often, we don't want to care: care is something we are made to do and care is something we are helpless to guard against, in both senses of the word; that is - all the ways we care and all the ways we are careworn by care.

We are born into an interwoven network of care, and finding out exactly what we individually care about amidst everything the family or the society into which we were born cares about, may be one of the great tasks of a human life. Care is the invisible shaper of our individual and communal identities. The power of care is demonstrated by the way it shapes our lives just as much by its absence as by its necessary presence. Being neglected as an infant can haunt us through the rest of our days: whatever the nature of our neglect at crucial thresholds of our growing, restoring our sense of being cared for or deserving to be cared for is also one of the timeless and often dramatic necessities of a human life.

Whether we are only seeming to care, or trying hard not to care: care, we are surprised to find, both lives and sleeps deep in our body at a seemingly cellular level, and is grown, matured and shaped from this seemingly hidden, involuntary core, whether we are conscious of it or not. Even trying not to care, we demonstrate that care is almost always there. Underneath even the most uncaring disguise care can surface and overwhelm us with the power with which it awakens, when it is suddenly, out of nowhere, discovered, found and felt.

Trying not to care is one of the great human defences against the vulnerabilities that care creates in our lives, the difficulty being that it is such a central part of our nature that we have to go firmly against our nature not to care. It actually takes tremendous energy to suppress what is central to our identity; trying not to care is the abiding source of much of our exhaustion in a human life. Care waits in ambush, engaging the cynic in constant watchfulness, lest it overwhelm their powers to suppress its greater powers. Care is the uncaring cynic's greatest enemy, but care never sleeps, care has been there all along, living at our centre and because of the way we are made, care will emerge in the end.

Care is our troubling friend, causing us heartache when we want to be solo operators free from any relationship, but also our constant, abiding and loyal companion, who refuses to go away and then, in the end, our unfailing teacher. In almost every tradition, caring deeply is seen to be the essence of being human; not to care, in all cultures, a way of being condemned as inhuman. Care is how we helped each other survive through the narrow, perilous, bottlenecks of prehistory; care is how we got here. Care led us, firstly to survive against mutual enemies, and then, astonishingly, in our greatest religious traditions, became our way of surmounting and overcoming the barriers by which we defined, named and kept our enemies at a distance.

The greatest thresholds of religious maturation have always been when our understanding of care suddenly grows beyond the boundaries of our self and our tribe, enabling us to extend it, even to our named enemies. Care is the path by which every human being and every society matures. If we allow ourselves to mature and do not arrest our faculties in senseless defences, keeping all the ways we care at bay, then care continually surprises us by the way it emerges from our depths, by how natural it is to our way of being, by the depth with which we increasingly feel it as we grow, but also, we realise, by how it leads us on, outlining as we go, the particular shape and outline of our own being, by how it seems to point unerringly to some essence in us that seems to love in turn, some essence in the world. In all human mythologies care is seen as our greatest gift, one that is somehow, always in the end, reciprocated, no matter how mysteriously and under what guise the gift may be given back.

Care is almost always connected to our close companionship with anger, the way our un-investigated and unspoken loves burst out of a human frame that has not learned how to carry the depth of affection we feel. Anger is the unspoken and helplessly destructive inability to feel the full depth of how much we care; caring therefore, rather than the anger and violence it might produce, is the essential emblem of our character. To pierce through the layers of our un-investigated anger is always to arrive at the source of why we care and who we care for, who we want to protect, and sometimes the awful lengths to which we will go in providing that protection.

Anger transformed into care and then spoken out loud, from a foundational level that represents the entirety of the depth with which it is felt, that is heard, shown and then demonstrated in the public world has always been seen as one of the great emblems of human maturity: an essence of our courage and a sure way of making ourselves free from anger itself.

We fall in love when we discover just how much we are willing to abandon what we thought were the boundaries of our self or our society, how much our care for another opens our previous sense of imprisonment. We open up a freeing road to the future when we confess that love, either in the wonderful reciprocal loving care we receive in return or in the more difficult freedom granted through realising our particular form of caring is unrequited. The difficulty of care is that, whether reciprocated or not, we are diminished if we try to care less, care knows we have to live with it, care doesn't care to change, care doesn't care whether it is requited or not, care finds its essence and its being in simply feeling the full depth of its love for another or for the world. Care just seems to want to care.

The depth and amplitude of our care, particularly as we mature always surprises and at times overwhelms us. We might only realise the full depth of an unconscious love at a poignant bedside, saying goodbye to a dying parent or a good friend. Sitting with them, the depth of our feeling suddenly astonishes us. Startled by the depth of our emerging care, we emerge from our defended indifference, realising how much we were implicated, how much we cared and were cared for; how much we were shaped and affected by another's life.

In parallel to its unfailing presence, care also carries its other accompanying resonance: the way we gauge and measure the constant sorrow we feel at being unable to right the shared pain of human existence. Care is intimately connected to our sense of powerlessness but also to our witness and our courage in showing love even when we have no answer to the sorrow of someone we love being hurt.

Care, without a healthy body and a healthy life to carry it, always wears us out, as in that beautiful word, so shaped, softened and washed by continued experience, *careworn*, where over time we feel the anguish of caring without having the power to offer remedies to those we care for - something we all experience, with those close to us or even with those far from us, in distant famines or unimaginable wars. To be worn out by care is to have lived too long in a state of helplessness; care in the end, always asks us for some form of decisive action, for some form of contribution, for a courageous demonstration of the depth of what we are feeling, even if it is not immediately welcome by those we care for.

The refusal to care is seen as a central tragedy in a human life and in all literature and religion marks the beginning of a downward spiral in the journey of a human soul. The actual inability to care, including the inability for self-care, is the thread that runs through many forms of mental illness and at the extreme end of the spectrum, the hallmark of psychopathy. Care might be the essence of our sanity and our humanity: care is the ability to see and celebrate the essence of another.

The measure of our care is the measure of our humanity and our shared humanity. Care is often marked by the line where we draw the boundaries of our greater family: in the Irish meaning of the word, we ask 'How are all your care?' a question meant to enquire of family and close friends, but unconsciously asking where we ourselves might draw that line: a line of questioning which if asked of a Dalai Lama, of a David Attenborough or a Jane

Goodall, might lead to an enquiry into the state of all humanity, of all living, sentient beings and every corner of creation.

CRAZY

is never as crazy as it seems, most particularly when it emerges from our own inner core, our heartfelt desires or our disturbed conscience. What seems crazy, is always to begin with, just our inner unrecognised, creative edge meeting our surprised surface life. Slightly crazy might be what all real creative or emotional breakthroughs look like and where they all have their best beginnings.

What we call crazy - the wish to create something unrecognisably new, the wish suddenly to tell the truth about something we have been hiding: the wish to be a poet, a writer, a fine carpenter, a dancer, a sculptor, a brilliant speaker: or anyone who wishes to make their work a singular gift to the world - is always perceived to begin with as unrecognisable, beyond the pale, and slightly crazed: crazy is what the new looks like before our surface mind has taken the time to name it or build a life around the unrecognisable.

On the inside, deep in the hidden wellsprings where real creativity begins, what we call crazy is actually emerging from something incredibly intimate, private, unrecognisable but absolutely germane to the way we are made in the world. We call it crazy because, to begin with, we can't find a way for it to join our present life; we can't find an easy label for what seems to be arising. We are each made in such a profoundly, particular alchemical way that the very particularity of what we have to offer as individuals is beyond what our every day minds can recognise. The particularity of what we are imagining cannot be comprehended by the surface mind whose job it is to name, categorise and smooth things over into generalities. To get down to this essentiality in each of us, necessitates an undoing of our surface persona and a willingness to experience a more moveable, creative world inside, which is resistant to easy names, and one we only misperceive as being eccentric and slightly mad.

Crazy always has an edge of wildness and indeed, fierceness to it, otherwise we would not call it crazy: and it is this moveable, creative, very fierce part of us, deep down at the centre of the way we are made, that is where we find the powers equal to the fierce, movable and seemingly crazy nature of the world in which we have to live. Our surface personalities abstracted from this creative centre, tend to become immovable and quite fearful when confronted with a difficult, constantly moving and overwhelming world. If we shape our identity totally around our ability to defend ourselves then this source that lives inside is often experienced as another threat, though this time, emanating from the inside. Turning away from both the world and from the equally wild centre that lives in us, we create a bland middle and a life in that bland middle that knows nothing of either.

The inner powers of the creative have always been perceived as the crazy rule-breaking part of us, and the most crazy part of that rule-breaking is that it would much rather fail at its own life than succeed at someone else's. What we perceive as crazy inside us can be frighteningly serious and frighteningly one pointed about its approach to life and to the expression of its own powers in that world. This 'take no prisoners' approach, can be disturbing to the parts of us trying to fit in to other's rules and other's lives, so that when we come intimately close to that part of us, by happy accident or by artistic or contemplative discipline, we often turn our face away in the very moment we first experience it. We become afraid of striking up an intimate relationship with what looks like a source of future trouble. We intuit quite accurately, that the road to brilliance lies straight through the land of trouble. The temptation is to trade unpredictable wildness for the safety of mediocrity, but the brave thing to do is to let a little wildness have its way with us, to see where it takes us. Stepping into what seems like the trouble inside us is the disturbing first footing of all new revelation, a new understanding and a new way we will find to go forward in the world.

Initially, then, we always turn our face away from that breakthrough, that revelation, that raw edge of vulnerability that seems like too much but that is now already holding a conversation with the world in a different way. This initial turning away, this refusal of the call - this unwillingness to be slightly wild in the presence of others - is just part of the cycle of maturation, and can be the first foundation of our growing bravery. Bravery needs self-compassion, because bravery always comes, to begin with, by not being able to be brave. The only question is: will we stay the course. Will we turn our face back toward what initially seems like our 'too muchness?'

Craziness, unmediated by good rituals, good disciplines, good routines or a good social life, always just stays in the realm of the crazy. We call it crazy because it is discombobulating, discomforting and subversive to our surface plans, but crazy is always asking us to transform it into brilliant. What seems eccentric and off-kilter inside us is simply looking for good disciplines, good art and good new forms of expression to find its place in the world. Some of these disciplines are grown through everyday routines we build in the midst of our troubles – good routines are always disguised rituals. When we establish good routines in our lives, they become rituals of investigation that take us deeper. Creative routines take a different form in every single life, and they follow very individual progressions towards their harvest: towards bringing our originality into a proper conversation with our everyday life.

Crazy can also be experienced through neglect, through not having touched what is both wild and nourishing inside us. Over time, not touching crazy makes us inhabit another less creative form of crazy. After a time, walking back into the part of us from which any form of brilliance or breakthrough can come, can feel as if we're bringing ourselves back from the dead. The longer we've neglected that part inside of us, the more disturbing, and wilder it might seem, when it does actually come back to life. Particular forms of un-lived energy have been living inside us all along, but inviting it back into the world, we suddenly see the stark difference between what we have always wanted to be and what we have unfortunately become.

Taking a step back toward what we have neglected in us because we have put it under the banner of crazy, can have an edge of rawness to it: something disconcerting, slightly distressing and subversive to the way we are living our every day life. We have to have sympathy, understanding and compassion for our surface personality – it is doing its best to help us survive and control things in a difficult, restless, uncontrollable world. Our personalities work overtime trying to contain energies which are always threatening to spill over or explode: from the very beginning of our life we have traversed all kinds of traumas just by being born, just by growing and receiving all the natural wounds we take on: physical and psychological, as we negotiate the difficult passage into adulthood. Crazy always seems like a threat to begin with.

Called or not called, recognised or not recognised, crazy is our inheritance inside and out. It's natural that our surface personality would be sceptical about the surprising nature of reality itself and by anything uncontrolled and equally surprising emerging from within us. The calming and quietening of the fearful, sceptical, controlling mind through a friendship with silence is the only doorway that opens our inner creative powers to the outside world. Practice, discipline and silence married to the inner wildness we call crazy, is always, in the end, what wins hearts and minds, including our own.

Our particular inner form of originality and craziness is always, every day, asking us to make a channel, a road, a way into the world that can take the form of a recognised brilliance: a brilliance that enlivens both our own life in practicing it, and other's lives by witnessing it.

The disconcerting, often overwhelming sense of the crazy emerging inside us, is a disguised invitation to get to know ourselves at a deeper more intimate level: an invitation to stay in constant touch with unrecognised sources just waiting to emerge, just waiting to find a form in which to be finally recognised. Crazy, is never as crazy as it seems, crazy is just the first sight of our unrecognised conversational, creative edge with an expectant, waiting world.

DEATH

happens only to other people, death will never find me. Death happens only to other people while I am alive; and strangely, death, when it comes, happens only to another person even when I am in the midst of dying myself.

All around us on the planet, every day, and in ways we cannot bring ourselves to think about, hundreds of thousands of people pass away, saying goodbye to their lives and to their loved ones. We walk in witness with death the longer we live, and we walk alone but often secretly speaking with those with whom we have walked and talked during their lives. But even as we mourn or celebrate those we knew and loved, we, unaccountably, live on - our hearts beating faithfully, looking on death as we do unconsciously on other people - as a strange form of miracle that can never be fully understood. Death is something that only happens to other people and that somehow and unaccountably, takes them from our daylight hours.

Death happens only to other people even when it happens to my self. I always become another surprising person the closer I get to the doorway of my own disappearance: if

I am conscious and able to bear witness to my going then in that disappearance someone else starts to appear, someone who I do not fully recognise who has lived for years beneath my busy daylight hours: the mercy in dying, if I am able to pay attention, is its stripping away of my previous priorities and my previous sense of self. The person who is dying is not the person I thought I was all along; the person who is dying is a new and unfamiliar being I am now getting to know as I go.

If I lose my wits before dying then death really does happen to someone else: if I keep my wits, then death becomes the beginning of a new friendship with someone from whom I spent a lot of time hiding over the years, someone I barely let breathe in the midst of my misplaced priorities and unneeded busyness: a new friendship with someone we realise we have neglected all along. Felt fully, in this new friendship, death becomes irrelevant or becomes just the magnifying, necessary background to this astonishing, delayed, getting to know.

How we live shapes how we die, with reluctance or with courage and almost always with a good measure of both, but dying well involves undoing the way we lived but did not fully live. Death happening to someone I am becoming allows me to understand who I was and wasn't in my life. I am brought to understand that what stopped me from living courageously is the same fear that will stop me from having a courageous death.

The approach to death is almost always felt as opportunity, refused or accepted, by the ones dying and by the ones at their bedside. Opportunity for confession, for forgiveness, for a blessed forgetting that releases everyone concerned.

Death, strangely and poignantly, becomes the opportunity to relive and to reimagine. Almost all people approaching death, once they are through the early torments of letting go, glimpse a radical simplicity they never felt they deserved or possessed; a simplicity that allows them, if they are brave enough, to make a new friendship with themselves, with their loved ones and with the world.

In our home, approaching the end, in those last days surrounded by family, or very often, in a hospital bed, attached to tubes and blinking graphs, with often, only the understanding hand of a tired nurse to hold us, we experience visions and dream-like meetings with those we loved and knew, often going back to childhood, or just as amazingly, forward, to a sense of being both welcomed and thoroughly forgiven. Palliative nurses tell us again and again, working at the bedsides of the dying, that these two dynamics of meeting and of forgiveness are constants, to be witnessed again and again. The near death experiences of those who temporarily die, no matter the trauma, speak of similar mercies; witness as in witnessing themselves and looking down on their own body, combined with serenity and even a sense of choice as to whether to stay or go. The person who dies is never the person who held on so grimly and so tightly and for so long. The person who dies is never the person who until now had never been given the chance to appear.

The one who dies in the end is the one who realises that, all their life, they unconsciously sought and quite often refused, an absent affection, and sometimes in contradiction, how much love actually surrounded them all along, or how through everything, they were held and helped by those familiar faces who bore witness to their growing, their struggles and their hard sought happiness.

No, the person about to die is always the one becoming another unfamiliar and newly astonished person, the one who can't believe what an extraordinary, ordinary miracle it all has been. The one who realises what a privilege it was, even to say no to love; the one who is astonished that they were willing to miss so much, or at times give so little and who forgives themselves for missing so much and giving so little. The person who dies is not the unforgiving person who came into the cancer, into the illness, or the hospital bed, the person who dies is the one who begins to forgive themselves in the light of all the forgiveness they suddenly intuit they are about to receive.

Death happens to someone else, to someone who appears at the end: to the one who has finally given up on many of the nonsense priorities that ran their days, death happens to this hardly recognisable, newly simple, vulnerable being now watching the evening light or hearing the gentle rain against the window, death happens to the person seeing the face of all humanity in the single pair of disbelieving eyes sitting by the bed: death happens to this extraordinary body about to leave the body that breathed itself so courageously and through all difficulty to come to this particular end.

We can all be assured that death only happens to someone else: someone I have yet to meet, someone I am about to meet: not me reading or writing, or listening to this essay, hoping, despite the title, that death will stay far away. Not me who wonders if I will be equal to all the saying goodbye, not me, who hopes above hope, that by technological wizardry, I can live forever.

It is an old fear, and a true one, that death always comes to find us: it's just that mercifully, and thankfully and even faithfully and consistently in the end, it does not really find us, with just a little help and a little letting go, death only comes to find the person we have always secretly, wanted to be.

ECHO

is beautiful and disturbing aftermath and as a word that chimes with its meaning, even carries its own lingering echoing response within its two short syllables. Echo is a word that carries the abiding, intuitive sense of the way the essence of our world is lived out through some form of foundational repetition and reciprocation: whatever we have to say, will be said again, in a slightly different way, by myself or by others, but whatever we have to say will also, somehow, be answered.

Echo tells us that whatever we give out to the world, will be returned to us, in ways we only half-recognize; what looks like self-repetition is actually a deepening and gradual revelation. In an echo, we are granted the ability to hear our own voice, in its truth and in its falsity. Echo also echoes with our intuitions around time: whatever we generate will come back to us in succeeding generations, everything sent away or lost will return, one way or another, in a beautiful, skewed, not quite symmetrical version of its own first issuance; echo is the sense and the deep unconscious relief that we will eventually, if we listen closely to far off things, be answered, and hope above hope, answered in the way we wish to be answered.

Echo is always a beautiful surprise and comes simultaneously from within our own body and from a reverberating, far-off somewhere else, arriving through multiple and simultaneous distances all at the same time. In creating an echo I stand for a moment at the centre of myriad variations of my own voice. I find I can become a creator of many conversations from one originating voice. As in my everyday life so in the experience of echo, one word from me sets off a multiplicity of responses.

Echo is also foreboding, the annunciation of absence; the empty room where children ran, but also, in that absence, the invitation to go back and meet, the memory, the loss, the life that once surrounded us but now beckons to be held in a different way.

Repetition through echo also reflects our need to admit things we could not admit to, the very first time we heard them. In Greek drama, when the gods spoke on stage, it was always understood that, heard directly from the god's mouth, the message was too overwhelming for those listening in the audience to take in. The words of the gods could only be comprehended and digested after they had been heard again, after what had been said had been echoed and repeated by the chorus. In the reverberating echo of the truth, the chorus mercifully steps the truth down to our level so that we may understand it and then through repetition, amplifies it to transform our lives.

Repetition and echo wrought well into speech brings mercy into human conversation. When we carry terrible news of loss to another, if we care for the person or for the person lost, we will always unconsciously repeat the news three times, in three different ways. Our voice echoes the actual pain of the loss and must draw an equally painful and grief-filled response from those to whom we have spoken.

To listen for an echo from the depths, in our thoughts, in our reading, or in our listening to the repeated drops of blessed rain after a long drought, is to live in the deeper parallels that transform a simple surface life, into a rich flowing, unconscious, multiplicity.

What I am saying on the surface is being said in so many different ways with so many different understandings throughout every level of my unconscious body. Your reading of this essay can be just as original as my first writing of it. Echo is as real as the voice that originally made it.

ECLIPSE

is what was seemingly there, just a moment ago, in the heavens, in our lives, in our understanding; now strangely and unaccountably covered over by some other, greater but previously hidden power. Eclipse is an everyday experience in a human life but death itself is the ultimate shadowing, a sudden presence in our shocked everyday life, suddenly eclipsing everything that was ordinary and making each ordinary thing, extraordinary. Eclipse is the end of the old and a literal foreshadowing of the new: a life bowed down by grief for the one we have lost, now perhaps, waiting to emerge slowly into the light, as elegy and healing.

Eclipse is the shadow of eternal movement overwhelming the powers of eternal presence. Eclipse makes a past of presence. The brilliance of the dependable sun even behind the clouds, now a shadow, an absence, even an opposite of itself. The way in a human life, one home is replaced by another, one marriage by the next, one person, astonishingly replaced by another, sometimes to our heartbreak, sometimes to our relief.

An eclipse denotes something beyond our powers to stop and something beyond our powers to understand. An eclipse can only be witnessed and cannot be interfered with, an eclipse is independent of our will or our worries. Eclipses have always been disruptive in a human life and in our mythological past, disturbing to whole cultures and societies: omens and representations of helpless distance and dislocation, but then mercifully, in hindsight, of necessary change.

An eclipse is the disappearance of something that was beyond our powers of imagination when it first appeared and is now equally beyond our powers of understanding in its going. The way a well-loved person unaccountably disappears from our life to be replaced only by the grief of their absence. The way a brilliant early light we carried in our youth gets covered over by the shadow of our care, of our responsibilities, of our exhaustion. The way we find our way back into the light again, sometimes by having to crawl on our knees in the absence of actual light or the light of any understanding.

Eclipse is the melding of past, present and future. Anticipation and lead-up become the awed now, then the witnessing of a gradual disappearance, then the fear and wonder of complete darkness and dissolution, all followed by the slow reemergence into a world which represents our future.

Eclipses give us a bodily experience of reemergence, of re-seeing and re-setting. I never really see or fully appreciate the sun until it reemerges once more as a burning, growing halo, from behind the moon, I never really understand how much I take for granted the heavenly powers that inform and invigorate my ordinary, extraordinary every day. I never really appreciate the light emanating from my son's face until it is far from me, eclipsed by distance, eclipsed by alienation, by neglect, until I allow it to re-emerge again through merely travelling to see him, through repairing whatever had set us apart, through the everyday miraculous simplicity of spending time together.

Eclipse is our end. At my death bed, some other power, beyond my understanding will move in front of my taken for granted comprehension and prevent me from seeing what I had only been under the illusion of seeing. I will be allowed, mercifully, not to see or to understand, I will be blinded so that I can see in a different way and carried by the great tidal movements of life away from the familiar: every eclipse I ever witnessed in the heavens will be but a rehearsal and a test of faith for some shadowed, long awaited re-emergence I could never ever previously imagine, and perhaps from behind the ebbing darkness another kind of light, another life, just beginning to show the bright, fiery haloed edges of a new and anticipated dawn.

END

is a word that stays satisfyingly true to its meaning by bringing itself to an end before it has really begun, by carrying the illusion of being an end in itself and by holding out the ancient but forlorn human hope for a word to end all words. The word denotes a decisive wielding of power in a human life: to bring something or even, shockingly, someone to end, is seen as a decisive, consequential action by a person, and carries an almost mythological power. To be someone who has ended something is to be someone who has taken the reins of their life at last, and who now has the power to take a new direction; someone who has brought to a satisfying close what needed to be closed a long time ago.

But mercifully, the word end also carries along, on its very short back, its own ancient, abiding and companionable spirit of contradiction: to announce that something has ended is to elicit an immediate and opposite reaction. We have only to be told that something has ended to immediately search in our mind for all the ways it has certainly not ended. We have only to be told that something is out of fashion to immediately bring to mind all the ways that it continues, against all odds, to abide in our lives and most secretly and embarrassingly, in our own wardrobe. Even those definitive and satisfying words THE END, read at the end of an old-fashioned film or novel, only serve to make us think of the new life this particular ending grants to all the characters whose lives we have been following to this last, definitive, arbitrarily drawn threshold of their lives. End almost never means the end. End only means we have reached the limit of our ability to track what is occurring. End is the word that introduces us to an intimacy with, an anticipation of, and even a readiness for, new beginnings.

End is never an ending in itself. End is transition, a temporarily visible seam in the invisible, making us, just for a moment, aware of what previously we could not see or hear or imagine and also, what is soon to impinge upon our surprised senses. Endings ask us to brace for the coming impact of a new and surprising announcement.

End is a merciful and useful word, not in its accuracy, but in its very lack of accuracy: it gives us the excuse to take a breath, to take a psychological rest in the illusion that something has now finished and that, miracle of miracles, something else has not begun, and that it may even be a good while before something new and stressful and perplexing begins. We wield the word more as a necessary excuse for temporary repose than as a real attempt at understanding what is happening. Human beings need endings whether they truly exist or not. End is our good friend, but end, of course, can never be an end in itself. The word loves its own illusory life in our mouths, while knowing all along there is no right true end in any of the endings we imagine we desire.

EVANESCENT

sounds just like the briefly passing essence of what it describes: something ephemeral, fleeting, fugitive, just beyond our grasp. Evanescent is a word whose beauty allows us to appreciate and touch for a moment what we can never halt in every poignantly, fateful, disappearance we are privileged to witness: the fall of white petals across a windscreen, the invisible race of wind that brought it, our breath suddenly spiralling in the cold interior of a frosted car; or the clouds racing over our unheeding heads in a passing rain storm, or within our minds and imaginations, the sudden, fleeting memory of an old desire, now no longer felt, but leaving a trace, an aftermath, like the way a constant breeze leaves a slight bend in the gnarled trunk of an ancient tree. Evanescent means something is here and then gone but also, something that has unaccountably changed something inside us, just by its passing presence.

The evanescent always leaves a trace in our memory: the first time and even the first micro-moment, felt deep inside our chest, in which we found the courage to tell someone how much we loved them: and in response, and with a lucky blessing, that passing shadow appearing and disappearing in the hearer's smile.

The physical sense of evanescence becomes more present and more poignant as the years go by: most especially greeting each new version of ourselves in the mirror and seeing in the faces of those we know, the arrival of age. The evanescent gives us a sense of all times living in one time, all faces living in one face: that image we might carry as a parent, of a young son, a stripling, light as the wind, running through the trees, now subsumed somewhere, beneath the bearded bulk of a grown man shouldering through the world - everything still there, everything still within, still there underneath, but somehow hidden from the surface - hidden and fleeting but still as much alive as it ever was. Evanescent is here but not here, there but not there, everything almost within reach but always, always a hairbreadth away from our reaching hands: like the way our memory changes the more intensely we give ourselves over to what we are trying to recall, the way our understanding changes in the revealing light and in the changing light of evolving circumstances.

Evanescent is a word that invites both a fierce outer attention combined with a practiced, inner watchfulness to follow the equivalent interior appearances and disappearances living inside us as a parallel to everything we are witnessing trace an arc on the outside. The evanescent calls us to be alert to the trace we ourselves leave through other's lives: or to feel the nature of our own brief, momentary appearance in other's eyes.

In our deep contemplation of what is astonishingly here and then just as suddenly, astonishingly gone, lies the understanding of how incredibly high are the stakes with which we play: that we do live a life in which we can miss things we never should have missed, that we can lose crucial tides that will never return again: our son's youth, a young wife's passing disappointment that if fully addressed, might have saved a marriage, the way our own briefly seen reflection in the mirror can transmit, just for a heartbeat, our unspoken but honest misery, and the way we can miss misery's invitation to self-understanding, covering our unhappiness with a false, reasserted and manufactured happiness, disguising our actual, more real descent into depression.

Evanescent speaks to the way we feel for even the briefest, minute seasonalities and sensualities of every passing, living thing: the hardly felt, whispering touch of another's hand: our first view as a child through the eye of a telescope, seeing constellations stretching away, into another dark waiting nothingness, everything always, always, appearing out of nothing and then in another kind of always, always disappearing, back into another kind of nothing but briefly brought to life by our seeing; our hearing, a nothingness somehow more inviting, more significant, by having for a moment, become an extraordinary, not to be repeated, gorgeous, passing, something.

Evanescent is a word that calls for brevity: for an essay to be here and then just as quickly gone, even perhaps, before we fully understand what has been said or before it goes on too long to try the reader's patience. Evanescent is a word that by definition, should never overstay its welcome.

Evanescent calls for us to be alert to every goodbye - to be, as Rilke said, 'ahead of all parting' - a person who can say that goodbye with as much presence and as much sense of arrival as we made our first inviting hello.

Evanescent is a word that carries a beautiful implied invitation to courage: to feel fully every last farewell that is asked of us. Evanescent is a word that implies we somehow already recognise and therefore are equal to and able for, every waiting - not to be contemplated - surprising hello and every accompanying heart-breaking, poignant and inevitable farewell.

FORGETFULNESS

is the mercy we extend to ourselves when we wish to preserve and protect what is precious. Forgetfulness is the gossamer web we weave around something we hid for safekeeping, so that it cannot be found by the world, but more importantly, so that it is safe from our own destructive hands. Forgetfulness is what we use to cover our heartbreak.

Forgetfulness is the web of self-enchantment woven by the mind so that it can continually assert its own false independence from the body, that with all its aches and pains, its vulnerabilities, and its longings absolutely refuses to let go of its belief in its own memory and its faithfulness to everything it has ever experienced. Forgetfulness is disbelief in our own unerring and foundational belief.

Forgetfulness helps us to get far away from a body that would gladly walk through its own despair and heartbreak rather than follow the abstracts of someone else's success. Forgetfulness grants us insulation and the illusion that we can live without anguish, without care, without the helplessness of a real, demonstrated love. Once we are forgetful, forgetful is how we want everything and everyone to be, so that that the forgetful world can share our own false surface state of happiness, and stop reminding us so terribly, of the very thing we hid from our own sight.

Forgetfulness is also the merciful measure of our distance from what must be remembered. Forgetfulness always tells us where the treasure is buried. What we want to forget or are trying to forget, and the very way we are trying to forget, is also the very way-sign, pointing us to the place we must go to remember.

Forgetfulness is the inverse state by which we come to understand that although we experienced something, we did not experience it with the full vulnerability to which it called us, that although we understood something we never understood the way it broke our heart so entirely and so thoroughly, that although we loved, we did not express that love in the way that was called for. Forgetfulness tells us that although some wound was delivered, and delivered decisively by an unknown blade, we could not allow ourselves to feel the depth to which it penetrated.

Forgetfulness, standing in the empty room wondering why we entered it and what indeed we entered it for, is the disguised urge to return to another room we left but never returned to: the holy precincts of the body that hold what the unanchored mind could never comprehend: the raw vulnerability of our primary, bodily experience and the life that it calls us to. Forgetfulness is the entirely understandable wish to let go of and forget what never should be forgotten.

FREEDOM

is desire, but felt in reverse; the sense of being wanted by the world and then the ability to respond fully to that invitation without impediment, interference or self sabotage; the sense that I am being invited by the world beyond any present boundary I have made for myself. Freedom's birthplace is a deep, spacious sense of interior silence in which I can hear invitations being made to me that will extend the outer boundaries of my sense of self. Freedom is the outcome of profound silence and the ability to pay attention in that silence. My individual sense of personal freedom is earned through the spacious allowing of silence which grants freedom to all those who come into my orbit. Silence is the key to freedom.

Freedom arises from seeing and hearing the essence of creation, of birdsong, of the heartfelt origin of another's speech and then allowing that essence to speak back to us with its own particular form of invitation and in its very own voice. Freedom is a radical sense of letting be and being let be. As Antonio Machado said: 'An eye is an eye not because you see it, an eye is an eye because it sees you'. Freedom is found in granting life to people and things other than ourselves that creates a mutually nourishing sense of seeing and being seen.

Our sense of freedom is always magnified by mutual allowing: a continual and surprising meeting of others and a release of all the ways we hold the world or our loved ones to ransom; freedom arises from a true meeting: the meeting that occurs when what is between what I think is me and what I think is other than me, come together in a conversation, an intimacy, a joining, intellectually, physically and imaginatively. Freedom can be felt in the body like new love. In our great mythologies, the freeing of another is always the ultimate demonstration of love. Freedom is self become other; become no self at all. In a real conversation, both sides find new freedoms, both sides are let loose and freed from any sense of self they have previously known.

Societal freedom is where my ability to be found by the world is not interfered with by others unless it hurts others: where I have the ability to make myself equal to whatever invitation is being made to me, either through a decisive, freeing 'no', an enthusiastic anticipatory 'yes' or the satisfaction of negotiating something extraordinary that lies in between. Societal freedom refuses to over-protect, and understands that true liberty is letting go of the protected self and allowing ourselves to be continually, disturbingly and delightfully, invited into new circumstances.

Freedom is always under threat: freedom calls for alertness, to my own or other's manipulations, from those who wish to assign names to me and rule me by assigning me a label that diminishes me and gives others an excuse to hold power over me.

Freedom always calls because freedom always lies, almost by definition, just beyond the frontier of my previous understanding. Freedom is an open relationship with what lies over the horizon of my understanding. Through silence and the deeper states of attention that silence allows, I see over and beyond myself to something that invites me into a greater world, a greater maturity. Therefore, even though I may not have reached the place where I feel freedom as yet, I have a sense of being free through the felt invitation to some new, unknown place where I may make a home.

Freedom is a state of deep attention and deep intentionality and is calibrated by my relationship to the breadth and depth of silence I have learned to sustain. In silence everything is allowed to speak in its own voice and in a register that invites me to speak back in my own voice. Freedom may be first understood through my being allowed to have my own opinions, but a deeper understanding of what freedom means arises when I realise that I live in a larger radius of experience without set opinions, that I am able to shape an identity through a freer more conversational identity that is recreated every day from the spontaneity of meeting and discovery.

Silence is the key I must find again and again in my life to open the door to a proper sense of liberty: in silence I am free to see that thankfully, things are not as I thought, and I am even freer when I discover that my thoughts and my opinions may be the least of me. Freedom is the anticipatory silence in which everything can happen and everything is allowed to happen in its own way and its own time. Freedom is felt like a broad sky and through silence I gain freedom not only for myself, but for all those who join me under that spacious, invitational canopy. Freedom is a radical letting alone, to be itself, of my as yet undiscovered self; and of every undiscovered self that tries in that broad amplitude, to come and meet me.

GUILT

is the wound that secretly carries its own cure. Guilt is the invitation to cure not only our own ills but the wounds of those we have hurt so thoroughly through desires we now realise were never fully understood, felt, or given room to breathe. Guilt is the measure of our distance from what we need to feel fully and what we need to transform through feeling fully. Guilt is the shared foundational binding experience whose exploration will ultimately heal every human conflict. Guilt is not something we need to get over, guilt is where we need to go.

Guilt is the first doorway to our foundational vulnerability and eventually our compassion, where we stand in trepidation at our ability to hurt others, and always in that ability, afraid therefore, that we are not worthy to enter and not worthy of understanding or being understood.

Guilt inherited from our past, rightly from our own actions, or wrongly from the misconceptions of others, is often thrust upon us when we were too young to understand. Guilt is what binds us to a past that cannot move on or mature or let us move on or mature until it is reconciled with our present attempts to make our unique, individual way through life. Guilt is the invitation to a real physical re-understanding of a traumatic past so that it can be brought to bear in a loving, fruitful way on our still difficult present. In guilt is the unrecognised, instinctual, ultimate first step to self-compassion, refusing to let us proceed whole-heartedly, and with a free heart, without including everything and everyone in our understanding, including our own helpless younger self that we hurt so badly and so thoroughly and almost always, all those left wounded in the wake of that helpless younger self.

Guilt is an unconscious emblem of our human bravery in refusing to move on too easily or too early. Guilt tells us that we feel something at such a deep level that as yet we have no full understanding as to why we have no remedy.

The first approach to guilt is always through mistrusting and regretting our desires and the way our desires always seem to hurt others so much. But guilt followed fully to its source always asks us, secretly and surprisingly, to embrace desire fully, to come to an understanding of why we followed our powerful beckoning impulses, why they made us unheeding of others but also how they opened certain difficult doors when we were helpless to open them in any other way.

The letting go of guilt is not to reject the body and its desires but to arrive fully in the body and learn to understand its greater wants and needs, and then to make those same desires an invitation rather than an imposition on others. The letting go of guilt is also to understand and forgive the body's inability to console our restless, lonely, unhappy mind and the difficulties that younger restless mind engineered for itself: trying to learn everything the hardest way possible, while giving others the hardest time possible. Guilt is the invitation to come to understand and thus forgive our previous self and then to look for proper means of reconstitution to those we hurt, perhaps in direct apology, but more likely, simply by bravely living a life where it is impossible to deliver the same wounds again, and perhaps, even more importantly, where we learn to protect and secure our world from the hurts we previously caused to others.

The full experience of the guilt we carry with us, properly felt in its full aching vulnerability, and in the full understanding of the powers we each carry to hurt others profoundly, consciously or unconsciously, is the very experience that will open our future again and enable us to have a mature and compassionate life free from the reins of our original sense of guilt.

Guilt is the ultimate invitation to psychological healing, always waiting beneath the surface of our every day actions and any false sense of self-satisfaction. Guilt is always compassionately waiting for us to catch up. Guilt is our heavily disguised friend. Either we will discover that there was actually no reason to feel guilty at all, or we will open that door to the ultimate human vulnerability, the understanding of how much we have hurt, and still can hurt those we love, and further, to understand, in the full sense of compassion that arises when the door of guilt swings free, even those we are were under the illusion, we did not love at all.

HORIZONS

are everywhere: both inside and outside of what only feels like our sense of self. The edge between what I think is me and what I think is you is as much a horizon as any line of mountains or that far dark line on the distant ocean. Horizon is the line between what we think we know and what we do not know, between what we think we see and do not see: horizons mark the threshold between the world that I inhabit and the one that seems to wait for me, between a world I can almost understand and what lies beyond the imagination of my present life. Horizons are creative, disturbing, invitational edges just by the fact that they exist.

Horizons between the known and the unknown are everywhere in our human lives, even when we refuse to lift our heads and our eyes to see them: wherever we live, the sun rises over a certain horizon and sets behind the opposite one at the end of the day, but often invisibly, because we have four thick walls surrounding us, set firmly against our understanding. Horizons are appearing and disappearing all around us whether we know it or not, even in my own mind. When I refuse to face something real and necessary in my life I stop looking at the edge between what I know and what I do not know; I close myself off from understanding by refusing to look at a necessary inner horizon.

Horizons are invitational edges between what is familiar and what must be imagined: the main horizon in my life is the line over which, imaginatively, my future lies. The line between the world I can perceive and the world that waits for me is also a parallel to my individual creative powers and to my sense of personal courage: my individual creativity is calibrated by how much I put the world I live in, into conversation with the world, beyond the horizon, I must live into.

Physical, outer horizons, are good for our individual human physiology, as recent medical studies tell us. It appears to be the case, that merely by taking time to gaze at a far horizon, with our head and our eyes uplifted and looking far into the distance, we are put into much happier physiological states of being than when we are looking down, closer to home, most likely into a screen: hence our need and thankfulness for a room with a view, for a walk by the ocean, for a sunset drive, or the calm that comes over us seeing the sun rise again over far mountains. The loss of distant horizons in our life is a recent phenomenon, our myopia magnified and our happiness curtailed by the multitudinous close-up screens, in our phones or on our laptops, that bring our heads down, that make our necks bent, that leave our eyes hooded, the beneficent physical horizons of the world lost to our gaze.

Horizons are never passive in their presence: consciously and unconsciously, horizons always exert a gravitational and invitational pull from afar - the salt line of the far ocean stretching away to infinity from our summer beach, a beckoning line far beyond our ideas of what a seaside holiday means; the distant line of mountains always calling from afar, even if we have never driven to visit them. More distractingly, and more personally, the far edge of invitation deep within someone else's, loving, seductive eyes, frightening and emboldening us, beyond ourselves, into another life and a commitment far beyond what our logical mind could ever contemplate. Horizons tell me I am all possibilities I can see or hear or even sense: horizons call on me constantly whether I ever reach them or not. No matter how far away, horizons call on me to live in a different way, wherever I find myself, most particularly, in this place now, from which I am viewing the next edge between what I know and do not know.

We tend to think of horizons as only being visible in the outer physical world but it is fascinating to find that we carry a horizon inside us that is just as real as any of the ones that reside in any of the far distances beyond our bodies. Spending time in silence we find that the invisible interior edge that lies inside each one of us is just as real, just as invitational and just as beautifully disturbing as any line between the known and the unknown that exists in the outer world of mountains, oceans or loving, seductive, captivating eyes.

The line deep inside my sense of self, between what I know and can articulate about myself and what lies at a foundational level inside me is always felt in a very physical way as an equally powerful invitation to exploration as any bold horizon out beyond me in the physical world. This interior line is the edge of my self-knowledge and the place from which my future life and any authentic articulation of the life arises. The interior line between what I would wish to say, and how I would wish to say it, between what I am and what I want to be, between what I cannot say and what I want to articulate or live wholeheartedly, is the threshold and horizon of my present maturity. Strangely, this edge of growing inner maturity is often felt as a line of resistance or immobility. What lies beneath quite often stays beneath the edge of my enquiry, the only way through this inner horizon is through silence and silently breathing into the resistance, into the seeming immobility of that edge: but true to the invitational spirit of horizons, what is immobile in me will eventually be what moves most in the end.

Looking down into my chest for heartfelt words, or intelligent, thoughtful perspectives, or words that encourage or embolden I always experience a line of resistance, an edge of immobility, a demarcation between what I want to say, what can be said, and what will surprise me in my saying it. This is my horizon between knowing and not knowing from which all good articulation and indeed, all good poetry, comes. Becoming familiar with that horizon and the increasing depth at which I must find it, as I slowly mature in my life, in my art or in my relationships with others, is one of the great invitational necessities of a growing life. This inner horizon might be called the edge and present limit of my self-knowledge.

Putting this inner horizon of self-knowledge and even the resistance to the depths which it hides, in conversation with the outer horizons of my present life, grants me the gift of creative expression: it gives me the ability to describe an everyday sunset with surprising originality when those inner and outer horizons meet in my words or my paint brush or even in my simple joy in being a happy witness. Uniting the inner limits of my understanding with the outer limits of what I can 'see' also puts me in a fruitful, creative conversation with my future. The bringing together of these inner and outer horizons is the basis of every authentically creative life.

There is another step. Bringing what lives below the horizon of my inner understanding into conversation with what lies beyond the limits of what I can understand in the outer world is the foundation for what we have always called mystical experience. In that meeting, all horizons start to move and disappear, any static sense of self needing an equally static world fades away and I experience the act of seeing and hearing as both a way I am shaping the world and a way I am being shaped by it at one and the same time. When the unknown inside me is put into conversation with the unknown that lies beyond the horizon outside me I experience a physical sense of radiance that I find I have always carried with me, emerging from below the horizon of my understanding. When inner and outer horizons meet and more importantly, when what they have hidden until now, meet, I walk in new pastures, I come fully alive, I walk, both alone and completely accompanied in friendship, by every corner of creation crying, 'Allelujah'.

HUMOUR

is a disguised form of spiritual discipline: an art form dedicated to the never-ending multi-contextual and multivalent nature of reality. A sense of humour tells us that whatever context we might have arranged for ourselves, there is always another context that makes our particular context absurd. Absurdity is the subversion of my present too-narrow belief and my too-narrow sense of my self: my appreciation of a suddenly revealed absurdity tells me, even in the midst of laughter, that I am willing to learn. Humour is my saviour. Shared humour equally appreciated, helps to save us both, shared humour tells us we are on the edge of discovering or seeing something new again, together.

A sense of humour makes us alert to the way we almost always mature through the many merciful doorways of humiliation, where any strange or fancy ideas we might have about ourselves are seen to be ungrounded, to have no basis in other people'e eyes. We may search for subjects on which we wish to be amusing, but actually, we ourselves are actually the chief centre of amusement. If we are equal to it, if we are big enough for it, if we are mature enough to take it: our flaws can be mercifully revealed to us through other people's laughter. Humour tells us not to take any names we have assigned ourselves or the world too seriously, humour allows a new and more lifelike sense of the world to emerge from what the laughter we hear from others, is identifying and recognising in us.

Humour brings us to the truer multi-contextual ground of our present reality, but also helps us to step off into the future from that very ground. Humour tells us that we can be more than what we seem, someone larger and more able for the world than all the smaller ways we have previously named ourselves. Through laughter, humour allows us to surmount and flow naturally over or around the edge of any straightening or besieging circumstances: and shared humour is a communal life blood, creating a shared approach to all difficulties.

Humour also calls on our discrimination because it is a sharp, double-edged blade that can so easily hurt us as much as help us. Those who have no sense of humour are rightly distrusted, and eventually shunned as being tedious; those who have nothing but humour to offer are known to be hiding something very important, mostly their own unhappiness. Humour can be used as a weapon to humiliate and shame another, humour can be used to actually imprison others psychologically and prevent their maturation. The way we are humorous or use humour is an emblem and a measure of our own maturity and most tellingly, our care for others. Being naturally but appropriately humorous is almost always a sign of psychological health. A person with a good, healthy sense of humour is always alert to calibrating the appropriate and perhaps even more importantly, the fine, illuminating nature of the slightly inappropriate. Humour calls us to alertness, to paying deep attention to who we are with and what for them, lies at the edge of the permissible and the impermissible.

Humour at its best is the passing on of happiness, the natural overflow of felt joy, the ability to lift another's spirits: one person laughing contagiously, or when we are lonely or alone, a sudden jolly arrival of companionable travellers, sweeping us up and on in the joy of communal bandinage. Humour can be both a personal and a communal gift: a lifting of the spirits that allows us to look down on our previous commitment to a necessary glumness and see just how much of that shadowed, narrow melancholy was of our own making, how much we refused to get over ourselves, how much we refused to be humiliated in instructive ways; to see or hear things new and surprising about the world and about ourselves - how much we refused to come out and meet the merciful, subversive, humiliating richness of our multi-contextual world that refuses and always has refused, our every, sober, puritanical no-nonsense attempt to pin it down.

ILLUSION

is as good a path to reality as any other. Illusions are merciful in that both the illusion and the person who held the illusion disappear, like magic, as soon as we see through them. Illusions show us the ultimate kindness by granting us new freedoms in the very act of their disappearance. Illusion is also my guard and my protection, my sturdy shelter and even my blindfold when I do not as yet wish to see or cannot face what is actually occurring.

Illusion is the invisible friend to my maturation: in the very moment illusion disappears I instantly become a different and usually, a slightly more authentic person. Illusions disappear only to be replaced by the next, necessary illusion. Illusions seem to know we need them and never go away, they are the very gateways to the next dispensation of our lives and a testament to our willingness to live with the never-ending heartbreak, surprise and trauma of existence.

Saying hello and and saying goodbye to illusion is one of the time honoured ways human beings learn what is real, and what they might actually want in life: human beings find out what they really want only by letting go of what they only thought they wanted, and by learning, seemingly, every time, the hard way, what breaks their heart, and therefore what they care most deeply about. Illusion is the beckoning hand to our future heartbreak and therefore to our self knowledge.

Human beings begin to learn a robust and necessary sense of humour through illusion, by constantly having to give away what was never theirs to have in the first place. A sense of humour is cultivated through the wry understanding that the generous insights provided by personal humiliation are always waiting patiently for us, just around the next corner. When illusion disappears I learn the most generous of all lessons, that most prized emblem of maturity, how to laugh simultaneously, when others laugh at me, instead of only years later, after the fact, after I have rid myself of the illusion that prevented me from laughing in the first place.

Zen masters tell us again and again through the centuries, that illusion and its subsequent disappearance is indeed a subject for helpless laughter. Zen teachers are at their hilarious, chortling best in those moments when their students are going through a genuine, traumatic loss of illusion. The old Zen teachers were deeply happy because illusion actually beckons us to a deeply renewed form of innocence. The loss of an illusion is not a loss of innocence; it is the loss of trying to sustain something that never actually existed, the attempt to hold on to something that never, ever belonged to us. The loss of our often very specific illusion is actually the regaining of the very specific form of innocence we will need to find again, the beckoning, very personal path we had temporarily lost. Perhaps the real hidden secret in the laughter itself is the fact that illusion, and the heartbreak of illusion, is the very path itself.

We make a true friend of illusion by realising that it is always there, always by our side, always visibly or invisibly present and that there is actually never a moment when we are not inhabiting a temporary state that will be replaced by, or that will mature into, a slightly larger, more generous, but equally temporary state of necessary illusion.

Illusion is our constant invitation to live in a new freedom by examining illusion itself. Illusion treats us if we are grown up and able to live with and through the continually disguised difficulties of existence. Illusion tells us that we are always just about to understand something we have spent a great deal of time and effort not wanting to know.

Illusion tells us that understanding is just a matter of time, attention and the constant willingness to risk our hearts being broken once again. Illusion teaches us that it is actually only a matter of time and circumstances before our heart is broken again, therefore we might just as well have it broken over something we care about, something that we care so deeply about perhaps, that it leads us faithfully and abidingly, through illusion after illusion.

Illusion is our constant friend and companion, sometimes visible, most often invisible, always beckoning, always with its hand on our shoulder guiding us to freedom, always asking us to understand something that, until this moment, and for good reason, we were deathly afraid to know.

IMMOVABLE

is what moves most in the end. Immovability is just an invitation temporarily refused. Nothing stays still in the end, not even our seemingly eternal stubbornness in refusing to move. Immovability is just a beginning: the first experience we have when we try to move on in the right way, but as yet, cannot find or touch any rightness within us which will enable us to stir from the place in which we have stopped.

In the human imagination, mountains have always been an abiding, ancient and rock-solid image of immovability, most particularly in the Zen tradition, but as even our ancestors knew, mountains move over time and move faster when they are carved and eroded by water. Mountains may be the representation of steadfastness but the moving river of time is what always wears away any immobility, either through transformative events or by arranging for a total drowning and disappearance. In the Taoist tradition, mountains and rivers were always seen as working and living together - the source of the river always hidden in the very heart of the mountains themselves - in other words, immobility always hides at its very centre, the power that will dismantle and undermine its own seeming inability to move.

To begin with, in the face of hard work or adversity, immovability can be our close friend, seeing us tenaciously through all difficulty: writing hour after hour until the essay is finished, refusing to go until the truth has been said, staying in our children's lives until they can stand on their own, sitting Zen like a mountain until the narrow silence flowers into broad and freeing insight. Immovability invites us to fully inhabit its foundational grounded-ness, but once fully inhabited, always collapses in on itself: one more essay written but now no longer carrying the necessary delight, the truth said only as a constant need to be right, parental love that makes children mere prisoners of their care; and the monk's habit and habits as much a costume to hide in, as the ones they fled for the monastery.

Immovability is one of the ways we make our sense of powerlessness visible and therefore touchable and addressable. Our stubbornness is always noticed, commented on, and even described in not so loving detail by our immediate circle. But a sense of immovability is also our opportunity for precise self-knowledge: our stubbornness and refusal to move is almost always concentrated into a visible and easily identified symptom: a fixed notion, a moral certainty, but also into a stomach that has become knotted by its tenseness and refusal to digest, into a jaw that has become clenched through refusing to speak, into the rock-solid neck that refuses to raise our head and our eyes for a greater view, and into our knit brows tightly bound by our emphatic repeated assertions of unassailable facts. Immovability helps us to understand and pinpoint exactly where in our minds, our imaginations and our bodies we are stopping the tidal flow of life and most especially, what strength we are using to hold everything back. The very act of feeling immovable around a point, an understanding, a moral law: tells us we are, by definition, reacting against something we have not fully understood, something that now has us in its thrall, something asking us for understanding by the very way it has brought us to a halt.

Mercifully, immovability is always just waiting to move. Immovability does not tell us there is something wrong with us: immovability tells us we are just standing immobile before the door behind which our rightness lies.

Immovability can be the spiritual gateway to a stillness that uncovers both our pain and our next progression. Like a physical injury to a limb, immovability means we are protecting something painful, something that does not wish to be touched until it is ready to be touched, something that is the essence of the injury itself. The injury behind immovability is always presented to us in a deeply physical way; felt as a lump in the throat or a paralysis of the limbs or immobilisation of the will. Immovability tells us we are in the part of our body or our psyche that has been mercifully defending us from the truth until now, and that in the very act of identifying it, we are at last, prepared to turn our face toward it.

Immovability properly identified identifies exactly what we need to touch. Immobility has been our guiding map all along, saying here: x marks the spot, this is where the treasure lies. Where you are stuck is exactly where you want and need to move. Immovability is a kind of patient, helpless waiting, a waiting for us to come back to the place where we first abandoned our lives. Immovability is always the very door through which we will look back and see it as the very way we came.

Immovability is often just the invitation to stay a while, perhaps to rest a while, perhaps to catch up with ourselves, perhaps to take time to be rightfully shy of where we need to go or even just to be merciful with our own inability to stir from where we are. Immobility might be our unconscious self-permission to get to know ourselves and our fears a little more, perhaps to understand why we have stopped along the way and what we are still afraid of.

Above all, our immovability invites us to touch the pain that first shocked us into our frozen state, and in the heart of that pain, feel the pulse that will set our fearful, immobile, hearts going again. Immovability is the invitation to the better, more moveable life I refused in the heart-stopping moment I first became immovable.

INJURY

is the invitation to live from the inside out. Injury is how we are shocked into discovery. Injury is in some form the fate of every human being and is always accompanied by a strange sense of its deeply, fateful nature, as if this particular form of incapacitation had been waiting for us all along, as if this injury now belongs to me personally, as a birthright, as much as the knee it effects or the leg it has broken. Despite the medical profession's general statistics around our accident or illness, injury always feels deeply personal and somehow redounds upon our identity and our life. Injury always makes us think in metaphors, and even mythic terms: every injured person, given time and space, always trials multiple possibilities around what they did wrong or what they must learn from this seemingly fateful blow. Injury, we suspect, is the beckoning hand to an understanding we can only respond to after we have decided to turn down every other way of learning.

The first shock of injury is in how much pain the body or the mind seems to make us feel at the moment of injury. The pain can be literally unbelievable and untranslatable to another. The body, we are surprised to find, wants to let us know in no uncertain terms all the agonising ways that some holy perimeter has been breached: that some wholeness is now less than whole or that some system is in disorder, no matter our wish to call it back to instant health and order. The underlying sense is that the pain and disorder will endure until some wholeness is restored. Injury invites us to explore the opposite of perfection. Injury tells us we are about to begin our travels through the unending land of the not-quite-right.

The second shock is in coming to terms with the ever-present nature of our vulnerability; a vulnerability that the injury has suddenly and unaccountably uncovered. Until we were injured, we realise, we always floated three feet above the ground of actual reality and often three feet above the realities of our own bodies. Injury refuses to let us take anything about our bodies or the world we have to negotiate for granted. Until we were injured we never understood the miraculous nature of the heart with its never-ending faithful beat until the day it refused to keep in rhythm; we never knew the incredible abilities of the knee to keep us lithe and upright until we sustained that slight tear in our medial meniscus; we had absolutely no idea that our bone marrow was and is the birthplace of our very life blood, until the word leukaemia spilled from the doctor's lips like a low, far-off verbal thunder stroke, breaking over our unsuspecting lives.

The third shock is that we have a completely different identity injured than we did when well. I am now a person who limps and is seen to limp, or who has lost an eye or a limb. I am a person whose hand trembles. I am a person who needs things I didn't need before: a crutch, a medicine, a watchful eye. Most tellingly, and most humiliatingly, I am a person who obviously needs help before anyone even thinks about how I can help them.

The fourth shock is how long the body takes and how much it needs to heal; patience is the sudden, necessary companion to injury and equally suddenly, injury asks me to have a different relationship with time and the possibilities of time and of what might potentially happen in a span of time. Time may heal all but I do not understand how much time that healing may take, or how my understanding of healing may change as time goes by. Injury humbles me in my understanding of time. 'How much time?' is now a question I know I can never, ever fully answer.

The fifth shock of injury is understanding how much we have to turn our identities inside out in order to truly bring about the healing we desire. Injured, I have the opportunity to realise that I have always treated the signals of the body as a nuisance and that healing involves me understanding how much my mindset is the real nuisance in the body's attempt to heal. Injury is an invitation into the very touchpoint of the mind, the body or the soul that was injured.

The sixth shock is the way injury invites me to contemplate my past and the way I have neglected my body in the past. Until I get to the centre of my emotional wound, I do not realise how much my childhood trauma asked for in the way of constant emotional protection: until I stationed myself in the very centre of the pain in my trembling knee, I did not really understand how many decades my knee has supported me without question, and how little support I had offered it in return; until I am injured, I do not realise how much I have been asking my body for non-stop performance, rarely giving it the rest or care it needs. The road to healing is the road that reshapes my previous relationship with the body.

To take care of my knee I need to put my consciousness at the very centre of that astonishing complex of bone, muscle, cartilage and fascia and have it speak back to the rest of me, telling me what it needs and doesn't want from moment to moment. I walk at my knee's direction instead of trying to make my knee correspond to some golden, abstract idea of how I think it should perform. Our first reaction to injury is to tell the injury to get better and as soon as possible, but we each of us know exactly how we react to being given imperatives about bucking up, getting over it and getting well. To begin to heal is always to begin to let the injury itself tell us what it needs; to lead us where it wants to go.

Until we were injured we did not understand how fine the line was between health and incapacitation, between being robustly independent and being vulnerable to other people's necessary help, and astonishingly at times, being absolutely helpless without that help.

Until we were injured we were under the delusion that we were secure from humiliation, and that, in the spirit of that word, we didn't need a well-developed sense of humour; until we were injured we didn't really accept that we were just as amusingly and not so amusingly vulnerable as everyone else.

Injury fully felt and fully accepted grants us compassion. Injured, we now know how easily mere mortals are overwhelmed by circumstance, how the greatest of reputations can dissolve with infirmity and how everyone else in our world deserves a measure of understanding just for the act of having being born into the illusory robustness of their all-too-vulnerable, fragile, accident prone bodies.

Injury is our unconscious enrolment in a fully earned form of hard-won presence, a doorway to compassion for others and a threshold of maturation.

We cross the threshold of maturation that injury provides only with our slight limp, or with our bad back: we enter only by holding our side where we feel the pain; we learn compassion only by helping the part of us that cannot help itself, and out of that we learn to help others who cannot help themselves. Through injury we reach an earned state of understanding, that we realise can often only be reached, by those who crawl across that difficult, hard-won line of maturity, determinedly, metaphorically or actually, on their trembling hands and knees.

INTIMACY

is presence magnified by our vulnerability, magnified again by an increasing closeness to the very fear that underlies that vulnerability.

Intimacy and the vulnerabilities of intimacy, are our constant, invisible companions, yet companions who are always wishing to make themselves visible and touchable to us, always emerging from some deep interior, to ruffle and disturb the calm surface of our well apportioned lives. Intimacy is a living force, inviting me simultaneously from the inside as much as the outside. Something calling from within that wants to meet something calling in recognition from without. Intimacy is the art and practise of living from the inside out.

To become intimate I must set out on a quest for something or somebody to be intimate with that mirrors and completes the place from which I started. To become intimate is to become vulnerable not only to what I want and desire in my life, but to the fear I have of my desire being met.

Intimacy is the raw living edge between what I think is me and what I think is you, experienced as a living generative frontier, calling me out from any way I have learned to hide. The need for intimacy is eternal and constantly emergent and always the best way we have of getting into trouble, both good and bad. Intimacy is a need felt so deep in the body that it actually seems like another body, a body, it seems, with desires other than my own, always waiting to emerge, to break through, to slough off any hide that prevents me from touching and being touched; through a newly emergent skin, through the suddenly opened heart, through the imagination stirred to action; through what I have written or painted or said or cried into the world. Intimacy is an oft buried need to meet another or the world suddenly met, through rebirth and new experience while reaching a deep foundational core of memory and rest all at the same time. In our emerging longing for intimacy, we intuit surface and core could be brought together in one seamless holding.

Intimacy cannot occur without a robust sense of vulnerability, and is tied to the sense of being pulled along in the gravitational field of any newly felt openness. In that new openness we feel as if we are pulled through the very doorway of our needs for something we desire deeply but cannot fully identify, partly because what we are about to identify is intimately connected with our own ability or inability to love. In a close romantic relationship we find ourselves vital and utterly present but also in a way that draws us with our partner into the heart of our flaws and our manifest defences. We feel the vulnerability of imminent refusal in new relationship; we feel nervousness in the still not confident hand trembling on the fretboard of a musical instrument, we feel a strange and instructive intimacy in our touching for the first time the lump in our skin that should not be there. Intimacy is the hand that reaches out to touch us through our own reluctance to touch and be touched.

The need for intimacy in a human life and in a human social life is as foundational as our daily hunger and our never ending thirst, and needs to be met in just the same practical way, every day, just as necessarily and just as frequently: in touch, in conversation, in listening and in seeing, in the back and forth of ideas; intimate exchanges that say I am here and you are here and that by touching our bodies, our minds or our shared work in the world, we make a world together.

Intimacy blossoms from mutual, welcome touch, metaphorically and physically: touch and touch-ability is the essence of our bodily incarnation. To be visible and touchable is to be both alive and able to survive, as an individual and as a species. Intimacy is our evolutionary inheritance, the internal force that has us returning to another and to the world from our insulated aloneness again and again, no matter our difficulties and no matter our wounds, where we join our need for rest and with an equal need for movement, our irremediable sense of aloneness with sudden need for togetherness. Intimacy is a human being holding the opposing poles of exile and homecoming together, making a cohesive world where one previously did not seem to exist. In intimacy we unconsciously or consciously hold the opposing poles of the world together. Intimacy might be the chief emblem of our humanity, the hallmark of our distinctive place in the world and the touchstone of our imaginative and social survival.

Intimacy always carries the sense of something hidden about to be felt and known in surprising ways; something brought out and made visible, that previously could not be seen or understood. In intimacy what is hidden will become a gift, discovered and rediscovered again and again in the eyes of both giver and receiver.

All of us were intimacy itself in our first coming into this world at our birth. We were conceived in the inconceivable: in the hidden, intimate mystery of conception, and just as miraculously, carried for months close to the midnight heartbeat of the mother who bore us. We were shaped by an indivisible closeness with our mother's body and then born through the incredibly intimate physical vulnerability that accompanies the circumstances of every birth, washed both by blood and many times by the accompanying tears of the woman who gave birth to us. Throughout our subsequent lives, we grew a seeming independence in the world while never ever leaving the anchorage of physical need and surrender that the vulnerability of our first conception and first emergence locked firmly into our bodies and our sense of well being.

All of us born into this world were born from others who were themselves born in the same physically intimate way: each of us have come from a long and unbroken line of intimate arrivals from the invisible and the untouchable, brought firmly and uncompromisingly into this very visible and quite often too touchable world. Incarnation and the adventure of incarnation is moving from the invulnerable and the untouchable to the increasingly vulnerable and intimately touchable, from the invisible to the visible, from the protected to the unprotected invitations we eventually begin to feel as we approach our inevitable deaths. To deepen intimacy we always need to deepen the invitation we are making to another and deepen the vulnerability we feel as we make it.

From birth to death we are touched - sometimes in ways that astonish us and sometimes in ways we cannot bear - but for all of us, the abiding theme is our proximity or distance from the intimate. We carry the hidden foundational memory of intimacy from our birth through the difficult thresholds of our maturity following our necessary, often heartbreaking adventure into an increased touchability, or we retreat and protect, keeping the world at bay with a necessary compensating vehemence that distorts our character and hides our gifts. We live in a very physical way in this world, no matter the abstractions of our safety-seeking minds; we live, right down to the mitochondria in our cells, in an extraordinary, miraculous instrument for continued intimacy we call a body.

Intimacy almost always at times, and almost against our will, takes frightening and overwhelming forms in a human life: the illness of loved ones, the sudden realisation that our own death might not be too far away, the pangs of heartbreaking, unrequited love: our need and our fear of intimacy is felt through an ever present almost volcanic force emerging from some unknown origin inside us, exhibiting to all and sundry, our previously hidden unspoken desires, flowing out against all efforts to the contrary, through our unconscious and conscious behaviours.

The basis of all drama in theatre, film or literature, is the inability of our controlling surface self to stop our intimate needs from emerging for all and sundry to see in the world. To become human is to become visible, while carrying what is hidden as a gift to others. Our greatest gift might be to touch and to be touched in turn, emotionally or imaginatively or physically: and in all the forms our dramas of longing take, the pangs of intimacy are felt as much in our distance as they are in our sense of closeness: distance makes the heart grow fonder, but also more helpless; we often create the most heart-rending scenarios in which we each play the starring role, demonstrating in the most obvious fashion, all the ways we distance ourselves, all the ways we immobilise ourselves to keep the need for intimacy buried, to keep it far away, to pretend it is something for others but something we ourselves do not have time for, do not want or do not deserve.

Intimacy is invitation met: in letting go, in undoing, in coming close to what we were previously afraid to close in on. Intimacy is intimately related to our sense of having being wounded, and the startling intuition that my way forward into life, or into another person's life will be through the very doorway of the wound itself. Intimacy invites me to learn to trust the way being wounded has actually made me more available, more compassionate and possibly more intimate with the world, by being opened in ways I never realised it was possible to be open.

Letting go of fear around my wound, or preparing ourselves to face new and greater fears through that wound are both intimate accompaniments to our experience and our understanding of intimacy itself. Intimacy is always calibrated by the letting go of or the taking on of fear. Almost always our fear is experienced as an intimate invitation to understand and feel fully our particular form of wounded-ness. Resting in helpless intimacy, in another's arms in another's care is often the act of healing the wound itself. Intimacy is invitation made and then met; almost always in the place I did not originally want to go.

Intimacy finds its ultimate expression in all the forms of surrender human beings find difficult to embrace: in allowing ourselves to be touched, in lying down with, in giving up with, in resting with, in surrendering to, in being nourished by, in wanting and being wanted by, in conversing with, in hearing fully or seeing fully or understanding fully. Intimacy is felt in holding the full spectrum of human pain and pleasure all at once: the physical ecstasies of melding and distance felt simultaneously.

Intimacy gives me a glimpse of a future in which I will live in many more dimensions than I live now; in intimacy I find that to enter these greater dimensions I have to give things up rather than take things on. Intimacy is the giving up of complexity and the anxieties that accompany complexity, of letting go, of undoing, of becoming simpler, and clearer and more humble in that same simplicity and clarity.

Intimacy is always close, always what lies beneath, always just one single step or world away from where we are now, but always, it seems, despite our fears and vulnerabilities, a step so full of promise, so full of fulfilment, anticipated or remembered, it seems to be worth everything our life or our surrendering bodies can give.

INVISIBLE

describes something living in the unseen but by its own strange definition, also something already half-seen: in our minds, or in our imaginations. The invisible world is actually one we have already tried to imagine, even hazily in our half formed daily thoughts, or by astonished physicists, in sudden and surprising detail. In our everyday life we are completely surrounded by the only half-imagined and the invisible: the way electricity flows, the way a radio can suddenly startle when starting up a car, the way electromagnetic spectra fill our rooms and feed our devices. Even the the grain of wood beneath our open laptop is compressed and held by forces we cannot see or properly describe. The invisible is omnipresent and relied on for our everyday practical lives as much as those few, almost irrelevant, tippy-top centimetres of the iceberg we call the visible.

Invisible is what lies beyond us, below us, inside us and even above us: beyond our sight, above or below the limits of our hearing or our imagination, inside that outer wrapping of our personality we call a self.

The invisible transcends our understanding of time. Many times the invisible reveals itself only after the fact: the love perceived in our mother's sudden harsh voice, years after we were scolded; our own youthful sins we could never fully articulate, now brought to understanding through the mature lens of our later years and then, as a triumph and almost beyond belief, a future once only intuited, now lived out on a daily basis.

The invisible is undertow: is gravitational pull - is always present, eternal invitation. In the human imagination the invisible seems to seek us personally asking to find it a visible expression. The invisible in a human life is understood as a sleeping singularity, about to become alive through multiples of itself: like a seed holds invisibility within its single skin, holding everything that will grow and shape its many branches against a future sky.

The invisible is always sensed as a particularity that will become a miraculous plurality. Like the very beginning of a thought first heard in the secret quiet of a human mind that then finds a voice, that then finds an outer conversation, that then transforms a whole society. What is not known now, or seen now will be known and seen and lived through in many guises. The invisible is the place from which our future births, the engine behind every visible movement we intuit is about to fill our days.

To be bereft of a relationship with the invisible is to be bereft of a proper intuition of the future. To have no perception of the inner horizon within us from below which, the invisible can emerge, is to be bereft of a necessary inner source: the invisible is the deeper well from which we drink and to live without conversing with the invisible makes us unaccountably thirsty for something we cannot quite imbibe through our readily visible world. The invisible is what keeps us safe from the illusory staleness that ensues when we take too literally, too seriously and too routinely, what we think we see.

The innate sense of the invisible that every human being carries beneath their deceiving eyes, their deceiving ears and the everyday, taken for granted deceptions of the naming mind is the foundation for our ultimate in seeking: the eternal search for love where love initially, cannot be seen or found. The invisible calls us to seek and then witness that love, miraculously arriving from nowhere, out of the invisible, out of the darkness, out of the great and spacious stillness inside us, to the simple light-filled life of being said.

IRELAND

has always just ceased to exist. The Ireland you are seeing or being shown is just a pale imitation of what went before, of what existed before you took the trouble to arrive at last: before time and innumerable other troubles wore it down and took it away, before the main characters in the local area passed away and left it bereft, before you turned up too late to experience the real thing, before you came to witness this present Ireland which bears little resemblance to the Ireland you came for. The music might be wonderful all right, but nothing to what it was in the seventies; the people can be lovely but spoiled now with petty materialism. The beauties of the west are now besmirched by 'Wild Atlantic Way' signs obscuring the very wild things you came to see.

Ireland always holds itself to high standards; but all of those standards have ceased to exist in the present and therefore, thanks be to God, cannot be met: Ireland is the beckoning hand of welcome and the wagging finger asking 'why did you bother' all at the same time. Ireland exists in the timeless and the untrammeled, but by the time you arrived at Shannon, the timeless itself suddenly seemed to have been made unavailable in a very untimely fashion.

Even we Irish ourselves seem to think we arrived too late, the high point having just preceded our ancestor's wading ashore, to supplant the rich culture of the *Tuatha Dé Danaan*. 'Romantic Ireland's dead and gone' said Yeats, doing his part to keep up the long tradition of saying goodbye: 'It's with O'Leary in his grave.' O'Leary himself might have been surprised to hear it, being in his own mind, the latest and most modern incarnation of the very old, long lament for what had gone before; for O'Leary himself, the real Ireland was long gone before even he had arrived and needed to be revived by Yeats.

No, the Ireland you want, you have just missed: it's not only with O'Leary but in all the other innumerable other graves that can be pointed out as you walk around the churchyards of the country, reading off the names and dates.

But then, the lament might be a subterfuge in itself; a way of preserving for ourselves, a land that so many people and peoples around the world claim as their own: a way of saying you can't really understand us unless you were here before, as we were here before in our childhoods or in our preserved imaginations, in our memories, passed down, voice after voice, generation after generation.

On the way to this deeper unconscious understanding of what it means to be Irish, which always presents itself to begin with, as no idea at all, we Irish ourselves have the pleasure of fishing for compliments in a back handed way: in a country where it is taboo to compliment oneself or one's country, the declaration that Ireland is just another, now developed nation, bereft of any projected romanticism can be a simple way of inviting visitors to prove the opposite: to protest, to point out that what they are seeing, or hearing or witnessing, is uncompromising, un-pasteurised, not to be found anywhere else, pure single-malt Irishness: the cool hand of reason on behalf of the intelligent unmoved contemporary Irish person, just the invitation for the visitor to form persuasive arguments, to try harder to articulate what we are witnessing and therefore and satisfyingly, prove ourselves un-Irish simply in our seeming to try too hard, in our forlorn attempt to overcome the bred-since-birth, local reluctance to be unique or celebrate any individual singularity in themselves.

Any arguments about what was then and what is now, ultimately fall off the sea cliffs that edge the land or are blown fully away in the sharp breezes off the surrounding brine: the very singularity of conversation in Ireland is actually the blurring of tenses, the understanding, half way into an exchange that what is being talked about subverts our present understanding of time itself, that the time you are speaking of now has no self-definition of its own; that what only looks like the past, is just as alive now as what masquerades as the present and the present itself simply an illusory trap, beguiling you into thinking you are on the way to that inconceivable, never to be reached place, called the future.

It might be difficult to found an Institute of Future Studies in Ireland, a title that goes against all logic as well as an intuition grounded in the timeless, or if this institute does comes to exist it could only be founded by American or English academics, or Irish who have spent too long in America, who then employ the deeply sceptical Irish who will then humour them by taking decent salaries while pretending to consciously think about the future in isolation. Ireland is a place where what has not yet occurred can only be spoken of in the same breath as what has so recently passed away. Ireland rehabilitates us into a proper, wide amplitude, conversational relationship with the underlying quicksilver nature of time itself.

Luckily, in the true, ancient spirit of contradiction, that seems to blow ashore out of the west, those who visit, who stand in a present bereft of anything essentially Irish, are soon about to become what we came to find in the days to come. For those who visit afterwards, any previous visitors, by definition, visited in the high old times, the good old days, the place others who come after us will look back to, shaking their heads at the mouldering ruins of the present that represent only a pale shadow of the glories that previous visitors, will be seen to have inhabited.

We can all rest assured that given time, and most often a great helping of time, everyone can become part of a timeless Ireland, it just can never be fully experienced in the narrow, un-nuanced and unimaginative now.

LOVE

is an impossible word, and one we should not attempt to try to write about. Love is a close secret we keep, even from our selves. Love is the unrecognised invitation in every relationship, romantic, collegiate and even, amazingly, the central unconscious spark that ignites a deadly fight between sworn enemies. Love is the destination for which we are unconsciously packed and ready to go, but love we find, is always the place that is disguised as somewhere else. Love takes us deeper while subverting what we imagined deeper meant. Love beckons to begin with and then in a quick change of mood, always begins to frighten. Love seems to push us away, but the step toward love or the step away from love is always the choice we make when we feel we are making no choice at all.

Love is a form of unilateral disarmament: an instinctual willingness for vulnerability that overwhelms our surface defences and at the same time, rids us in a frightening way, of the need for defences at all: love is frightening, exactly because it overwhelms and disarms us, takes us apart and strangely, simplifies us into something more real, more grounded more generous: something simply un-recognisable, even as we are overwhelmed.

Love is what we feel deeply but can never name in our sudden radical simplification, love's job is simply to rename us, and then in turn, to rename and redefine every part of our lives, eliminating or downsizing all previous priorities, turning our world and our selves, inside out, and our outside, in. Love is contagious and always leads to other forms of love. Love takes us across the planet by plane and across boundaries we never even conceived we wanted to see or explore, bringing us to ground in strange cultures; asking us to fall in love with the unfamiliar as much as we fell in love with the person who brought us there. Love is an origin and an arrival all at the same time, giving the journey between origin and arrival, a new, surprising and burgeoning meaning, beyond our ability to name or understand.

Love can only be refused temporarily: and only to our confusion and our loss of vitality: love has a sense of humour and likes to make us pay for the times we refused its invitation: but love's patience only stretches so far and is merciless in working to break apart and destroy the identity that refuses love.

Love waits outside us, calling us on, but love the trickster is also already inside us, calling us inward to some other foundation that is no foundation at all but some elemental flow, some inner correspondence seeking some equally moving inviting symmetry in the world: the glimpse of a face, or the sound of a voice calling us out, the curved back of a violin asking us to lift the instrument for the first time and play, even when we can't: to kiss when we are shy of kissing, to see and confirm that grateful look in the eyes of someone we have helped through our work, confirming our love for the work itself.

Love is never just human centred, and even when centred on a person opens up the birdsong in the broad sky around them to new hearing, the branches of the silhouetted trees to a new seeing, the breeze to a fresh scintillating sensitivity on the skin. Love always wants to lead us back to its origin: to the foundational embrace of creation: the clouds racing across a rain filled sky: a leaf floating back and forth against the solid pattern of dry-stone wall. Love is the bright path made like a comet's tail, emerging from below the horizon of our understanding, hidden deep in the body, out through the eyes and ears and the imagination and then over the horizon and far limits of our outer understanding. Hence the bright eyes of someone seeing the object of their love: the scintillated ears of someone listening to a Saint Saens violin concerto, the concentrated mind of a physicist busting out gloriously obscure equations across an empty blackboard.

Love is merciless because in its raw elemental form, it is non-negotiable, it does not ask for reciprocation or for our affections to be requited, love just wants to take the path to a deeper and greater love and will burn away in its fire any who will not follow its uncompromising way. Love, we are afraid to discover, just wants us to love.

Love asks us to be courageous as it travels through all its differing and sometimes heartbreakingly unrecognisable seasons: to take time away from things that once we loved but that now to our heartbreak, imprison us, to take time to understand a newly shaped form of our affections, or to learn anew, how to keep our affections alive. Love asks for radical re-imagination - to see when love must offer deep friendship rather than romance, or bravely, to bring a relationship in its present form to a different form, to grant both sides new freedom, to learn the difficult art, of bringing things to a loving and affectionate end: to learn the art of generous endings, so as not to carry un-harboured resentments: and then to find a way for love again, even through separation.

Exile from love and the absence of love is just as much a path to love as love itself: the divorce, the fading of original affections, the carrying of resentment and the nursing of unforgiving sentiments are all invitations to a greater understanding and even a new future for our original love, a love we thought was only possible in a specific form.

The fire of love, fully felt, is the daily experience of living in a world that is better than anything we could ever have imagined in our previous longings. Love is the ultimate arrival that makes every previous longing and even every previous absence of love, even all the damage we caused along the way, merciful, understandable and even necessary.

Human beings have always been unconscious and heartbroken apprentices to mastering love in all its many forms, and we follow this apprenticeship in the midst of even the most ordinary, seemingly loveless, life. We should be astonished by love's abiding everyday presence in our hearts and minds: and to find, even to the consternation of hard bitten accountants, vast areas of our economies driven by the urgencies of love and the gift giving and unneeded luxuries that arise from its unyielding grip.

Throughout all epochs of recorded time, we should be surprised, although we never are, that we never tire of talking about, celebrating or lamenting the pangs, splendour and squalor of love, requited and unrequited.

In all our songs, our poetry and our dramas both ancient and present day: it's always love, love, love, one way or another. Every serious young philosopher and poet is always existentially disappointed at the threshold of their literary maturity, to find that it is, in the end and in fact, just about love.

Love is the very atmosphere from which we breathe and from which we make a meaningful life or even to our continued astonishment, a meaningful work - and in the end - no matter any difficult symptoms we exhibit, love seems to be the one and only cure for the pains, the vulnerabilities, the contradictions, the drama and the continued never ending heartbreak of love itself.

MOON

might carry the most evocative combination of vowel and consonant sounds in the English language, calling us to imagine its round reflecting white orb, even as we say its ancient name; exerting its gravitational pull on our voice and our thoughts, as if emanating and emerging through the extraordinarily long sound that lives at the centre of that initial soft 'm' and the half spoken 'n' that begin and end its passage through our mouths. Moon is an extraordinary word, equal to the astonishing celestial body it calls to mind: it is a word that carries the circular sense of subtle celestial change, representing that overwhelming sense of presence and part presence, presence and non-presence that the moon itself inhabits in our lives. The sound in the word *moon* is like the moon itself, coming and going while giving a reassuring sense of being eternally present.

The moon sails forever, and has sailed forever, through the dark sky that lives inside us as much as the night sky above our house. We have grown and evolved on this planet from the simplest cells to the extraordinarily complex creatures we are, in an intimate parallel with our waxing and waning satellite. Living on this earth has always meant living in an abiding, awe struck companionship with something both overwhelmingly close and too far away to control. We have always lived, half reverently, half resentfully, at the whim of that imaginative, physiological, psychological power we call the moon.

Living on this planet, we everyone of us live at the moveable edge of a powerful conversational triad: the earth's grounded gravitational pull that gives us a solid place to stand: the sun's strength of light, allowing us to live, to see and be seen and even voluntarily move toward what we see, and then the moon's other ever shifting, half-hidden gravitational power, making itself known through the tides or the tides in our bodies, always pulling us away from any fixed point to which we try to hold, always pushing and pulling us through powerful fields of attraction that seem to mimic and embody our own desires, whether we wish to be pulled or not, whether we wish to have those powerful upsetting tidal desires or no.

In the human imagination the earth might be where the sun illuminates everything we need to see and name, but the moon has always embodied the task of carrying the unnameable, and lives according to its own hidden urgencies, which in our daylight hours are forgotten or only half revealed. The sun illuminates our way, the moon carries those powers hidden in our present that will fatefully influence our future.

In the human imagination, the moon has always represented an alternative life; another body of deeper parallel laws than the ones we follow in the full light of our rules-based days. The moon tells us we are subject to powers far beyond our ability to summarise or understand. In the human mythic inheritance, the moon is the body's susceptibility to other bodies, our helpless attraction to what calls us beyond our present life; no matter how perfectly arranged that life may be, the moon embodies our deeply felt response to the greater, physical, tidal pulls of existence.

The moon works on and within the body in a way unregistered by the thinking mind. The moon and the moon's pull on the body cannot be audited or fully accounted for, the moon works both by stealth and overwhelming, silent power. We intuit that the moon's unconscious power exceeds the narrow consciousness we bring to our daylight ambitions. Mythically, the moon has always been intuited as carrying instinctual understanding while the sun only illuminates what the moon already knows before things come to light. The moon's tidal pull on us has always been felt as subversive to the desires we seem to hold at our lit, well-managed surfaces. Human plans are linear, made for the light of day and that light comes directly from the sun in a straight line, but the moon's power is tidal, a constellating force, pushing and pulling everything, outside and inside, right down to the tiniest mitochondria in our very cells, working away within our inward parts. Though the moon seems to hang above us in the night sky, the moon is always intuited to work from the inside out.

Whether we live deep in the barely lit countryside with views of each and every phase of the appearing and disappearing moon, or in the reflected light of garishly lit cities, where we glimpse it only at its fullest, as a startlingly white orb, suddenly suspended between buildings, the moon runs through us just like the mighty tides it draws back and forth across the planet, changing and moving both our inward sense of presence and the way we shape our every inward, onward way through each and every one of our outward sun-lit lives.

The moon's effect on our individual human physiology is well-documented: its effect on human social restlessness, waxing and waning with its own appearance and disappearance: but the imaginative visual presence of the moon in the sky and in our lives, is a power that steers our lives beyond any physical phenomena. The complete and utter disappearance of the moon for between two and three nights every month is marked deeply in the human imagination. We mark the three days and two nights when there is no moon in all of our great religions and mythologies: Jesus sojourning three days in the 'bowels of the earth' before the Resurrection, Jonah three days and three long nights in the belly of the whale: three days and three nights to solve the great riddles running through our fairy tales. Three days and their accompanying nights are the times when no answers can be found, when we must live through the night on the night's own terms, when any answer would be the wrong answer, any direction we decided to take would be the wrong direction. The moon has always instructed us to live without easy answers, to stay friends with our disappearances as much as our many appearances.

Though historically associated with the feminine and the inward mysteries of fertility and conception, the moon has for thousands of years been just as much the guiding deity of innumerable, overwhelmed crews of male sailors and all those who suffered the ocean's tidal dramas as much as it has been for those who followed the mysteries of the moon-goddess Diana. The moon has guided and scolded the tidal lives, the departures and arrivals of the half-respectful, half-frightened masculine psyche as much as the feminine. In the age of sail, sailors even expected to be paid by the moon, by the lunar month, thirteen, not twelve times a year.

The moon in its hidden but abiding power both motivates and transcends sexuality in its half-secret half-understood grip on our attempt to live lives independent of the underlying but overwhelming power of our desires. Diana the goddess of the moon beckoned but also killed those who responded to her invitations. Whether we occupy only the upper reaches of our naming minds or the deeper reaches of what swirls below our everyday consciousness: the moon is our half-passive, half-overwhelming companion, moving and swaying the hidden and the oceanic in our lives whether we travel on its troubled surface or swim within its restless ever-moving currents.

Spoken or not spoken, moon is a word that will always - like the body it represents - have its way with us, carrying us helplessly toward or away from known and unknown shores, inside and outside, always there, always asking us to face some hidden reckoning to which we never gave enough importance. The moon is sometimes seen, sometimes half-seen or unseen in the heavens above our wondering heads, always brooding and breathing, ruling our night skies through its presence or absence, while living clandestinely in every cell of our bodies, sailing through the ink dark night, forever above and forever below the limits of our understanding.

NAGGING

is love un-listened to, from both sides: the helpless nagger and the equally helpless, nagée. Nagging is something both sides want to turn away from, something both sides would rather not experience: but something that is also an abiding and ancient necessity, when, inevitably in every long-term relationship, love meets powerlessness: nagging is our way of knocking on a door when those living inside most need our help but refuse it, or when we ourselves neglect again and again to ask for help: nagging is necessary in every committed human relationship: because nagging is the way love tries to survive when it feels it has no other way.

Nagging is the way we signal our helplessness but also our underlying commitment not to go away; to stay in the fray; and in the only way we can for the moment, by knocking on their door: a testament to our tenacity in wishing unconsciously to find a proper form for all the things we feel we have to give, all the ways we care and all the ways we are not received, none of which, we know as yet, how to properly deliver or articulate.

Nagging is the merciful way we make contact and keep contact when it seems no contact can properly be made: when we do not know what to say or how to say it: when we do not know how to invite or be invited. Between intimates in romance but also in close friendship, nagging is the emblem of our inability to care in the right way, and the way, at times, no matter how sincere we may be, our love is often helpless to help.

Nagging may be the real but helpless signature of a real but misaligned care and affection, but also, from the other side, from the side of our being nagged, our own real and misaligned resistance to listening. We are nagged quite often because we are not really listening, to another, to our conscience, to what is good for our health, to the courageous, beckoning path we refuse again and again to take.

Nagging has probably been in our human lives and our human evolution since the dawn of time, when we were held too firmly and scolded, while our mate finished the grooming we probably asked them to start. Almost certainly, nagging cannot be eliminated from relationships of close affection: nagging is almost a true sign of real commitment, any long term commitment always runs into the dynamic of helplessness: helplessness to be heard, to be understood, to have the other understand. Nagging is a way of keeping some kind of contact when all other ways seem to have broken down.

The dynamic that nagging represents, followed sincerely and observed sincerely, teaches us in the end how to give and receive proper invitations. In nagging I have the possibility of hearing my own voice and all the ways I ask for impossibilities, but also the way my voice, in the reaction it creates, contributes to them staying impossibilities. Nagging asks me to find the real invitation and the real vulnerability in the invitation that lies beneath my surface attempts to contact the other person.

Nagging is intrinsic to all real relationships between real, flawed human beings; even Zen masters nag their students, most especially their best students. As a Zen student or a Zen lover in an intimate relationship, if you are not trying, not fully present, not caring, you yourself might not be worth the energy of a good nag. From our side, we intuit that if we are not at least a tiny bit nagged in our relationships the other person may actually have given up caring.

Human beings eventually become lonely without the real care that a good bout of nagging implies: to live in a truly nag-free environment, is often to live without friendship, without intimacy, without real, collaborative, collegiate, creative relationships. Nagging is ever present and can even be deeply satisfying: we even take satisfaction in nagging people about their nagging.

With only distant, Zoom-mediated, often antiseptic, nag-free relationships, we are left, thanklessly, to nag ourselves, which is actually the most irritating, most repetitive, most annoying and unchanging form of implied nagging and criticism we could ever experience. But even then, in nagging myself, I am also looking for a way to make a proper invitation. I will not go out the door for my run, unless I get beyond threatening myself: with ill health, with weight gain, with accusing myself of sheer unadulterated sloth, until I actually invite myself to remember and re-experience the eternal, invigorating essence of what it means to be fit and healthy.

But whether we nag or are nagged, nagging is by implication a diagnostic of real intimacy: nagging says I have earned the right to nag and be nagged: I have been given permission to observe and to care at close proximity and therefore to speak from that proximity, no matter how unskillful my speaking or my observations may be.

Nagging is transformed when the judgment and critical observation are turned through the helpless vulnerability of care into proper intimate invitations combined with a deeper, more silent, less judgmental attention to another.

My ability to transform nagging starts when I start to deepen my own ability to relate in companionable silence, and pay attention from that silence. In that silence I start to understand why it it is so difficult for me to change and therefore why my loved one also finds it so difficult to change. In the dynamic of haranguing our own selves, we begin to look compassionately at all the reasons why we are digging our feet in, why we are so resistant, why we won't listen to ourselves or change ourselves. Nagging is a mirror to our ingrained inability to listen to a wiser perspective, no matter from where that wiser perspective issues. Nagging asks me to let the other person radically alone, and therefore to allow myself the same freedom.

Nagging is that heavily disguised, beautiful but un-listened to, invitation to a better life we all want to receive: always despite ourselves, and always, always, always, always, despite the other person, trying to be brought out of the place where it is presently hiding. Nagging is love, just love un-listened to, from both sides.

NOW

is presently overrated. Now is not what it was and is also never what we think it is. There is no power of now: now does not have any power by itself. Now belongs as much to its past inheritance, to what brought it about, as it does to its just-about-to-happen future. Now is not where we are supposed to live, isolated from the poignant and maturing illusions of memory or the joyous lineaments of anticipation: 'now' does not exist without its astonishing past nor its dreamy, not-to-believed future: Now is a word that in the last twenty years has definitely got above itself. Most tellingly, and as a final condemnation: now is a word that has lost its sense of humour. Saying we should live totally in the now is just as amusing as saying we should live totally in the twelve-and-a-half minutes ago.

The call to live in the now is always accompanied by a grim form of dressed up puritanism. People who want us to live totally in the now want us to join their particular understanding of now, and very often to pay for the privilege. The now we are called to, we are told, is the only place to be, and not living in the now disqualifies us from entering the particular heaven on offer. The narrow cleaned up definition of now we are being presented with, hides the actual, underlying, raw and uncontrollable, subversive, not to be defined experience that lies behind the word. No, now is a word that does not like to be corralled or led by a singular understanding. The more emphatic our use of the word, and the more controlling its attempted meaning, the more it escapes our understanding. Now, like us, occupying the present just as we would like, needs to be left alone to be its multivalent, moveable, unnameable self.

Now is a much more talented word than we allow it to be. In all its moveable forms it offers a much wilder, less governed more realistic understanding of time than its confident use as a narrow imperative indicates. Now is a word we often use as an imperative. We invite others into all kinds of 'now' not realising how many different invitations 'now' can make, according to the differing understandings, prejudices and cultural leanings of speaker and listener. There is the familiar 'It needs to be done now', of the work place, which can mean everything from this instant to next Wednesday, depending on what is being asked of us. In Spanish 'now' always has to be modified if we really want to know what kind of now we are talking about. German has four everyday ways of saying 'now' - all having different meanings. In Yorkshire or Ireland - 'Stop now,' often means the activity in question shouldn't have occurred in the first place and therefore carries within its meaning, echoes of past injury; 'Stop now' invites us to examine the past. The inclusion of the word in 'Nowadays' is often just a prelude to a speaker's underlying conservatism and reluctance to move into the actual now, as in, 'kids nowadays'.

Then we have the famous phrase 'Be here now', which might have been the start of all our present troubles. The request to be in the now, always sets a question as to which 'now' we are actually being invited into. Again, in Yorkshire or Ireland, particularly Northern Ireland, the word 'now' is actually used to mean that things are only just about to start, as in 'now then' when something is placed in our hands, or in Belfast, when the waitress puts breakfast on the table with the single word, 'now', breathed in our ears beyond the time any self respecting 'now' has a right to exist, and carrying as it does, at least five hidden vowel sounds that are almost undetectable and unpronounceable by the rest of the world. In Belfast the word 'now' lingers long into the future.

Now is a word that asks us to rehabilitate our understanding of its true power and to use it rarely and sparingly; always with a sense of humour or with our tongue firmly in our cheek. Now is a word we have made unequal to what it actually includes and needs rehabilitating mostly by letting it alone to be its most multi-faceted self, so that it can have a better future than we have allowed it, that is, as an invitation to the timeless, in which past present and future can live together.

Entering the timeless 'now', the isolation of any present moment disappears, bound as it is to every other moment that has occurred and and every moment that will occur. Now is an experience where past, present and future disappear as separate entities and join together again as one whole, turning us inside out and outside in in the process. Now is always more than we can presently understand. Now is never just now. Now is a word that can allow us to experience ourselves as a wave form that carries origin, arrival and present illumination in one whole.

Only our precious, always changing, always maturing memory and an equally growing sense of anticipation for the future can make the 'now' fully possible.

OLD

is always surprisingly new to those actually growing older: the stranger in the mirror a mortal testament to the rigours of the journey, we seem to have undergone. In the daily and surprising newness of recognising we are old, one thing we know for certain: that stranger in the mirror is not a true outer representation of the new, inner, fresh life, still being born, far inside us.

The fact that we are surprised by age might be the most amusing, surprising and even comic fact of all. Advancing age, whether we are thirty-five or seventy-five, is always extraordinarily fresh in its appearance - we keep meeting ourselves as if for the first time in entirely new guises and disguises. Age, despite its age-old dynamic, always does take everyone by surprise, both in the mild shock of seeing ourselves, as if for the first time, in the passing shop window but also in how others deign to treat us, addressing not our true inner self but a self they have assigned to the outline we make, to the lines in our faces, to our silhouette, to certain behaviours and misconceptions we are also troubled to think, we might be unconsciously reinforcing.

Age is an accusation in the court of mortality, and there is a solid, foundational part of us that knows for certain we have been unjustly and purposefully framed and that we stand before both judge and jury, perfectly innocent of the crime. We look into the mirror and do not see a proper representation of our inner selves, we actually accuse ourselves as others accuse us, we see someone who seems to have committed a felony on our behalf: seeing our reflection we feel we are subject to guilt by association with this person looking back at us; we see the reflection of some shifty and untrustworthy individual, given to ageing far faster than what we experience on the inside, but someone we gaze at uneasily and guiltily, knowing that we have somehow unconsciously aided and abetted that same process. Our outer, older self is someone we may have accompanied from the inside out, but someone we know only at a strange distance.

We see someone in the mirror, buffeted by wind, weather and heartbreak; who has made a difficult journey, we see someone who has suffered through making that journey: we see what hurt them and we remember what might have worn them down over the years, but in that reflection we see nothing of the new complexion continuing to emerge from within, that we intuit, is our real self - a self that seems to still carry the necessary innocence for the journey, waiting just beyond our present grasp.

Old is never us, and the intuition may be a true one. Even in the vulnerabilities that occur approaching death, the mind and body revisit and re-inhabit the younger body and the younger self we once were, shrugging off, in that elemental memory any disease or any burdens recently shouldered. The essence of a human life might always, at every age, be just getting ready to be ready.

Every new measure of our increasing age, whether eighteen or eighty, seems to demand a new inhabitation of youthfulness, a way of looking forward independent of outer form: a sense of standing at a new threshold, an innocence without which, our future life withers under trembling fears that tend to be dressed up as a wisely gathered cynicism.

Old is a necessary shedding, not only of the need to have a younger, outer athletic body, but the shedding of the way we have understood age itself. We may anticipate being 'Old' as denoting a closing down, but the merciful perspective is that we are only closing down because at our mature core we feel everything more keenly than we ever did in our younger, immature and immortal days. Age, eldership and an ever-keener physical memory of successive heartbreaks, combined with the bodily understanding of our increasing vulnerability, can have us, old as we are, experiencing life like a heartbroken adolescent once again.

The only cure for personal heartbreak is to hold a greater context larger than ourselves, a greater context and, we might say, a greater sense of humour, and thus the puzzling accusation of being old asks us to learn to live again as a different kind of witness to the disappointment living in our reflected face, or in all the many faces of our society. Seeing the disappointment ingrained in our own face we learn compassion for what others carry carved into theirs, we understand at a deeper level, the inevitable heartbreak that others are powerless to help, and how many times, we have been powerless to help ourselves.

Seeing ourselves in the mirror we come to understand a deeper sense of witness, and the way our companionship and compassion needs to be extended to others beyond the lonely face we see looking back from that same mirror. We start to invite ourselves out from behind the surface image and we begin to invite others out from behind theirs. We magnify this invitation and make it all the more powerful by refusing to give others, or ourselves, easy, gratuitous advice.

Ageing is our apprenticeship to both increasing presence and increasing disappearance, at one and the same time. Just as we could never fully understand in our twenties who we would become in our fifties, we come to know, whether we are believer or unbeliever, that we will never understand fully who or what we will find on the other side of our approaching disappearance. We give up on what is easily visible in order to go on in a different more invisible way.

Age and maturity at their most admired, always combine to create a fine sense of humour about who we are, who we were and what we actually contributed to others; a gathering sense that even with a massive reservoir of cash we may have built in our retirement accounts, the rest of creation might very well be relieved to see us go earlier, rather than later, in the universal program of events: to make way for something less guarded, less defended, less abstracted and a little more willing to be a miracle that risks itself amongst all the other miracles of life. It may be instructive to think that creation seems to have taken a magnificent risk with our first appearance on this earth and might be just that little bit disappointed, once we stop risking ourselves in a manner equally to be admired.

'Old' transforms, transmutes and transfigures desire. Eros and attraction do not fall away with age, desire stays alive, more intriguing for the quicksilver manner of its transformation. The axis of attraction only moves, from the outer complexion in its attempts to call in other bodies and other lives, to an inner axis of attraction, an inner complexion, calling not only for physical union but a meeting with a greater invisible body that we intuit has awaited us all along; a union that is an inherited birthright, a very physical and very non-physical sense of belonging to the ageless.

Those desires we often followed growing into life - the car as a signal of our glamorous powers - the unused boat as something we could constantly mention - the second home that kept our vacations just as busy as our home life - are all suddenly seen to have been, not doorways to adventure but shields against any true, inner discovery, and all, in the end, too narrow, too ungenerous, and even in the grand perspective, quaintly absurd. We realise that many of the objects we thought of as the natural gifts of an earned maturity were simply new toys appropriate only to a series of second infancies.

Age without maturity is always the second helplessness of a childhood much worse than the first one. Age, combined *with* maturity not only holds childhood's core understanding of play being far more important than any particular toy, but most especially, age combined with an earned maturity keeps youth's precious and visionary relationship with the future alive; most especially our ability to think generously of other, younger people's futures, and even to be generous with futures we cannot as yet fully understand.

Youth has the burning need to travel on from the here and now, 'old' has the possibility of understanding that no matter where it finds itself in the world, 'here and now' is the biggest, most challenging, and most interesting journey of all, demanding everything for our proper arrival.

No matter whether we are called 'old' or not, no matter our chronological age; at thirty, or even, in our not too distant future, at a hundred and thirty, in the midst of our life or at the shoreline of our death; at the very centre of all the edges and unattractive horizons that have us hesitating at the word 'old' there can burn the rose fire of an inner compass pointing to a new true-north. A compass hidden for so long, but now, despite every outer difficulty, disability or disappearance, able to blossom in new and strangely youthful directions.

'Old' is not a state that replaces the word 'young', but a fierce and uncompromising invitation we have earned, exactly because of our imminent disappearance, to the unfolding, eternal, and ever-surprisingly new.

PUBLIC

is what we all, privately and secretly, are, whether we want to be or not: whether we are overly extroverted politicians or classically introverted poets, or more likely, like most of humanity, somebody who lives on that long and interesting spectrum in-between.

The essence of human consciousness is the consciousness of being seen and of being heard and of being found by things other than our self. Alone or with others, I make my identity at the edge between what I think is me and what I think is other than me; therefore all identities are by definition public, and are shaped by what we are witnessed by, whether it is by the face of a single loved one, my own face in the mirror, a conference crowd, a sea of voters or a far, beckoning horizon of mountain and sky.

Even if I live alone, I arbitrate my sense of self through the stranger who speaks back to me every morning as I rub my eyes in the mirror, by overhearing myself speaking to myself as I quietly do the dishes or by the recognition offered me by my semi-indifferent cat or joyful dog. What lies inside us must always find some way to find and be recognised by a life outside of us or what is inside us dies at its birth. What we see outside of us always asks us to find an inner articulation inside us that is equal to what we witness. My identity lives in eternal conversation, spoken or unspoken. I am never, ever alone, I have a public self, even on a solitary walk in the woods: even in silence, something is hearing me hearing the birds, something is seeing the way I am perceiving the trees, something is always in parallel, just as alive as I am. I walk in mutual witness even when unwitnessed by other human beings.

My sense of self is mediated half by the way I see myself and half by the way I am seen; half by what I hear myself say and half by what others think they hear. More interestingly still, my sense of identity is a meeting of two extraordinary unknowns, what is inside of me as hidden and unspoken potential and what is waiting for me as a potential hidden by the world. To become human is to become visible while carrying what is hidden as a gift to others. To become fully human is to become equally appreciative of all the gifts emerging from the hearts and minds of others.

Our public nature is our ultimate vulnerability: being seen means being touched and therefore, perhaps, being hurt; being public holds the possibility of being hated and humiliated and even more disturbingly, being openly loved without feeling we have deserved that love. The public nature of being human, in a family, in a community, on the pages of Facebook, in what we write or say, or sing, or even grieve, calls for a constant bravery that is not bravery for its own sake but a bravery that is the emblem of our inner world attempting to integrate fully with the world that stands as witness. One of the great triumphs of a human life has always been intuitively understood as the ability to create a seamless open road that leads from their origin in the deep privacy of our inner life to the public world where those gifts will be shaped, given final form and made ready to be received.

The giving and receiving of gifts in public, in the presence of others, take ancient and abiding forms in a human life: the form of a large orchestra, of a theatre filled with people and actors: the form of political ideas accepted or rejected, and of terrifying invitations to speak in front of a crowd; by all my ways of being hospitable and receiving hospitality, from a quick drink with friends to being offered a seat at a lavish banquet. In more humble ways I shape my public self simply by walking into a crowded family kitchen. Perhaps we should acknowledge our ordinary daily public appearances, our constantly being watched and witnessed, by bowing to our partner at the sink or lifting our hands for a welcome from the kids as they do their homework at the table, even if we create nothing but laughter we would temporarily make our eternal visibility conscious instead of eternally unspoken and unconscious.

The arena of public invitation, whether as participant or witness, is the edge where a human being feels most vulnerable and most afraid, but also where they can most flower and where they can feel most alive, and most deserving to be alive. Being public is always a test of the generosity of our spirit. There is no inner life that does not cry out to be witnessed, that does not long for an outer expression of what it intuits but has not yet brought into being. Our public life is not the opposite of our private life, our public life is simply the other necessary, nourishing, life-giving half of our abidingly private being.

RELATIONSHIP

might be a word that deserves our sympathy but not our willingness to use it so frequently. Relationship is a word that lacks magic: trying to describe the place where we want the most magic, but a word, that in the end, can lead us back to magic, through the very way it represents almost all the opposites of what we wish to experience.

Relationship is a word that might, if it could speak to us, admit to being difficult, unattractive and hard to say; a word that is not much use when what we actually desire in our heart of hearts, is the raw intimacy we first felt in initiating our romance, our marriage, or our creative collaboration with another.

Relationship is a word that has never been equal to the mysterious alchemical joining or the physical intimacy we try so hard to make it represent. Relationship is the guardian figure standing by the doorway of the temple of what we actually want. The word relationship is a word we often wield unconsciously as a weapon, keeping at bay what we most long to attract. Relationship is a word we use a great deal when we have actually given up on what it represents. The very overuse of the word relationship about our relationship, tells us that we are grieving what it once held for us, mourning our loss or our underlying possibilities for the future.

It is no surprise then, that relationship attracts the equally inadequate word 'work' to join with it to give us the illusion that sheer effort will allow us to solve its heart-breaking difficulties and dilemmas. Relationships we have been telling ourselves for decades are hard work, but real relationships almost by definition cannot be the hard work we so fashionably insist they are: relationships that are hard work are actually relationships that are already coming to an end, at least in the form we first met them. Relationships that are hard work are relationships that against all possibility use the same part of the mind that first confined and condemned us to mutual imprisonment to try to keep us both alive and free. Relationship is a word we think is key to our happiness, but one that does not fit the lock that will free us. Work and relationship are words that measure our distance from what we want: 'working on our relationship' is what we say when we are already far away from what was once intimate and close.

The very use of the word relationship in a romance, a marriage, a collaboration is the first annunciation that we need to move on, from the relationship itself, or from the way we we have allowed ourselves to move into distance and abstraction.

Relationship is the word I use to abstract the real presence of my physical and emotional pain. Relationship might be a first doorway to broaching the conversation, but is helpless to articulate the depth of vulnerability from which we need to speak or the brave invitations we need to make, both to ourselves and to the other with whom we are so desperately trying to live, and live again.

Relationship asks us not to use the word relationship. Relationship, once said as a first stepping stone to addressing our difficulties, asks us to find more particular, more invitational and vulnerable words able for what we desire. Relationship as a word is always asking to be replaced by other words; ones that live in the grieving body, that live in our secret longings and in the physical intimacies equal to what we suddenly know we are missing and know we have been missing all along.

Relationship is a word that has no magic, but in its very lack of magic, tells us once we get beneath it, that it is magic we want and desire again. Relationship is a word that compassionately calibrates the measure of our distance from that secret and unspoken desire, every one still carries, sometimes far within them, to fall head over heels in love again.

REVERIE

carries the same, beautiful, half-awake, half-asleep sense in its sound as it does in its dream-like meaning. Reverie is a rare and neglected state in our times, asking us to pay attention to simultaneous, inner and outer horizons: with a rested bodily depth and with a broad listening amplitude. Reverie is an antidote to much of the over-focus, over-delineation and branding of our identities, most especially in an age where we are drawn like moths to a flame, burned and distracted by the internet, from one state of narrow focus to another.

The combined state of rest and broad diffused attention that reverie implies, and the luxuriant sense the word communicates, invites us to inhabit our bodies, our intellects and our imaginations simultaneously, where neither the mind, the body, nor the imagination are given precedence yet all of them are felt and inhabited in deeper ways that are not possible when we attempt to focus on them in separation.

To be in a state of reverie is to inhabit multiple layers of our consciousness all at once, to be fully aware of every bodily internal feeling while hazily hearing and seeing every ambient sound and sight: to be present in this time now while inhabiting the timeless, employing the mind to re-interpret the future and even re-imagine the past. The word reverie recalls to each of us, the luxuriant sense of rest, we might feel in front of an open fire, perhaps even nodding off, of the body rested and resting deeper, while all the time acutely aware of the sound of rain brushing against a window, the logs crackling and the sound of children playing mutely in the distance. A hammock by the ocean, inhabited without a phone, and rocked by the arriving sea breeze holds the same invitation. Reverie is our ability to take it all in, all at once without making a job of work or a task out of taking it all in, reverie is our multivalent, multitalented ability to connect to all levels all at once and all without effort.

Reverie is always despised by those do not like the broad freedom it grants us from other people's wishes and other people's control. Those who wish to control other's lives and to make them conforming members of a classroom, an office or an army do not like the way reverie puts us beyond the bounds, not only of the controlling minds of others, but also beyond the part of our own mind that is easily manipulated by others. Reverie and day dream puts us beyond manipulation. Reverie has always been the foundational imaginative corner stone of every child's life, and every child's sense of safety, free from the rules and regulations of oppressive adults.

Reverie is the refuge and sanity of all prisoners, and all who are confined, justly or unjustly, by walls put into place by others. Little wonder our working environments our educational systems and the present unimaginative views of the mental health industry, deplore reverie, asking us to sacrifice our ability to advance on a broad front for constant, unimaginative short term focus: a focus that can easily be manipulated by others. The medical community and drug industry wielding their diagnosis of ADHD might be the most guilty in medicalising, stigmatising and monetising reverie, ignoring all the ways that reverie is a viable, alternative way of being present in and to the world. Our stigmatisation of reverie has large costs on the sizeable portion of the population that does not conform to a smaller but more powerful percentage of people whose priority on constant focus and constant linear achievement makes a kind of shadow dictatorship for us all.

Reverie must be reclaimed. Despite the fact that approximately fifteen percent of the population doesn't share the majority's short term emphasis on constant focus, and despite the fact that this must have conveyed some kind of evolutionary advantage on the broader human population there is apparently, according to the drug industry, the doctors who serve them and the coercive majority, something wrong with every single one of the twelve hundred million people who do not wish to participate in their coercive, overly focused world.

Reverie is subversive to control, a subtle form of rebellion against other people's priorities - in China young adults are 'lying flat', refusing to join the exhortations to focus and 'eat bitterness', in Japan, many young people are refusing to leave their rooms: both are signs of helplessness, but both are push-backs against coercive societies asking them to be one way when they want to be another. Reverie is often our refuge and our sanity, and when we come out of our rooms and combine it with an outer, active life, it might be the very best kind of sanity.

Reverie might be a refuge from other people's priorities, but it is also a rewarding state in and of itself. In reverie, parts of us meet, join together, converse and even heal, that our isolated intellect is powerless to enjoin. Ideas, understandings and direct physical apprehensions of others form in the cross fertilisation and conversational cross-currents that flowing, dream like states of reverie provide.

Martin Luther King's power lay not in the fact that he had a plan: his power was much more conversational, much more invitational and all the more convincing in that invitation, because he told us, out of a reverie, that he had a dream.

RICH

is how we all want to be, and rightly so. Wanting to be rich is our unconscious parallel rehearsal for a state of spiritual enlightenment. When we long for riches we long for all the qualities associated with a full and generous spiritual maturity.

In wealth, we see spaciousness and ease, the ability to rest; we see and long for a life where we do not have to try so hard, where we feel power over all of the things that seem presently to have power over us: with riches we want the ability to be surrounded by beautiful things and to have the leisure to appreciate those beautiful things, we want to reach a state where others perform daily and repeated acts of kindness for us, but act as if they are not being paid to do them, and above all, where we experience in every welcome, a seemingly automatic respect.

Being rich, we imagine, will allow us to travel and to travel comfortably with that magnificent comet's tail of natural charisma associated with great wealth trailing behind us. We will be rich and therefore we will be somebody, and that somebody will always be creating a dash in other people's lives. When we do arrive in other people's lives, being rich allows us the ability to do the right thing at the right time for the right ones, to be a constant source of gifts, to be seen, in short, as a generous human being.

All of the many qualities associated with being rich, listed above, are laudable attainments and surprisingly, every one of them qualities historically associated with a form of spiritual enlightenment. Equally surprisingly, every one of the qualities above: natural charisma, a generous disposition, a constant sense of the miraculous able to happen, in our own and in other people's lives; a spirit that naturally invites help from others might be more possible with just a little money, rather than too much money, with just enough rather than too much. Which begs the question of how much money might be just enough money in my life; just enough where I am not held hostage in my life by the need for more: a question that is radical and transformative and rarely asked in most human lives.

Actual riches have always been more than tricky for most human beings, and our stories and mythologies are full of gleeful scenarios of the pitfalls, traps and havoc that wealth creates in a hapless human life; in fact, our inherited understandings of wealth in every culture tell us that too much in the way of material riches might not only be in the way of what we imagine being rich might grant us, but an actual obstacle to maturation, and even a step toward the inhuman.

Firstly, we know intuitively that inherited wealth, or a sudden windfall, or riches won too easily, always touches a core foundation inside us that feels undeserving, an undeserving core that drives us unconsciously into scrapes where we give away, or are embezzled out of our money, or alternatively, embarrass ourselves with investments where we might just as well have thrown our money to the four winds. This amusing and bemusing dynamic is repeated again and again with lottery winners and sudden surprising recipients of unexpected inheritances. We humans, strangely, always seem to want to get rid of what we feel we do not yet deserve.

Secondly, any strivings for earned riches, on the other hand, take tremendous effort and a long-extended focus over time, in which narrowing that focus day by day, becomes a practice in itself, a practice that also shapes the narrowing of our identity in a day-by-day, parallel way.

Despite the neglect of a son, a daughter, a spouse or even a circle of good friends who slowly seem to fade away, we can actually become proud of practising being a person with narrow priorities, and even celebrate in the morning mirror having become a person of pronounced but narrow views. We fall into a form of amnesia so that the earning of further riches constantly substitutes for the greater qualities we originally thought riches might provide. Becoming rich through our own effort where riches are the main goal, often involves a lot of counting and the sobering fact is, the part of the mind that does all the counting is the part of the mind that is least concerned about our happiness.

What we each practise on a daily basis is what we each become. After a lifetime of trying, or even succeeding at becoming rich, we almost always find we do not have the spaciousness of mind to spend time contemplating all the beautiful things we might have collected along the way. We might have learned to walk right past beauty every day on the way to the next most beautiful thing. In our long sacrificial journey to riches we might even find we have lost interest in anything that does not somehow continue to remind us, that we are, after all, rich. Under all the glittering surfaces we might find we are becoming exceedingly predictable or tedious, swathed as we are, so luxuriously, in our charismatic, but foggy halo of wealth. It is a cliché, but a cliché that seems to be a cliché because it is so true, that almost all billionaires I have met (there are marvellous, rare exceptions), despite the astonishing opportunities for growth in their lives, have the emotional intelligence of tedious, privileged adolescents.

Astounding wealth always puts us in danger of apprenticing ourselves to astounding arrogance: I assume, because of my untold, unfathomable wealth, the right to presume over others, and over other's lives. None of us is immune: make me a billionaire today and you will not be disappointed, I will demonstrate tedious, privileged, adolescent behaviour tomorrow or sometime very soon. Being rich has always been an impediment to paying attention to other people and particularly to other people's pain, being insulated by riches often prevents me from feeling a way into the core of another's life, to the sorrow of another's life, to being able to demonstrate real compassion for that life.

For those who do reclaim their memory, their spirit and their freedom after becoming rich, the greatest gift of being rich is always a sudden understanding of the obvious: just the spacious, radical simplicity of not having to worry about money itself. Which begs another rewarding question: why not be practical and start by worrying just a little about money, just exactly enough but not too much, from the very beginning?

'Just exactly enough' is an old Zen practice that as a question asked over time becomes a reward in itself. By practising a radical simplicity, by doing good work at the essential frontier of self-corroborated reward; by paying attention to beautiful things, that we might not have to own, like the hills or the trees or the horizon of the sea, why not, from the beginning, practise being generous in ways that need presence and imagination rather than ones that take large amounts of money and the endless hours to make that money; why not practise doing the generous thing now with the modest amount you have, where modest means always asking for real imagination to magnify what is modest, why not practise a simple quiet nobility, in a way that garners automatic respect, from the very start? Why not practise all the qualities of being rich right from the beginning, even when we have very little money?

There is absolutely nothing wrong with wanting to be rich, it's just there are two very different ways of going about it. One that takes tremendous effort, a certain kind of amnesia, a focused and often exhausting ambition: very often cut-throat competition, a great deal of day-by-day counting, a necessity for constant self-justification and the steady but inexorable, narrowing of priorities.

Then there is the other way to riches that asks us to practise the art of being rich right now, before actually going through the possible degradations of trying to become rich: this other way of practising being rich before being rich, might be more practical and more attainable, and could be started today, with just a little courage and a little practice. Given that the young wish to be rich but after becoming rich simply wish to spend their money on becoming young again, we could start when already young or just when we feel young at heart. You never know, by a happy confluence, money and wealth might accidentally come along with it too. Rich is not just how we want to be in the future, rich, as we all come to understand on our deathbeds, is how we wanted to have been, all along.

As the Sicilian Briton said, fifteen hundred years ago, speaking to the whole spectrum of humanity: 'There are three kinds of people in this world; the rich, the poor, and those who have enough'.

ROUTINE

is the way we worship fully at the altar of the timeless. Routine is the way we step down from what is absolutely extraordinary into the miracle of an ordinary day and an ordinary hour. Routine is disguised ritual.

Routine is not the routine word it has come, so routinely, to sound. Routine is how we disguise our rituals of attentiveness: and like all rituals, routines are a way of enriching our relationship to a puzzling and sometimes overwhelming world or keeping that same fierce world at bay. I drink my coffee at the same time by the same window every morning to appreciate the tiny miraculous nature of its taste or contemplate the extraordinary nature of my changing daily realities, or I drink it feeling besieged, I drink it hurriedly, not quite ever fully present but also not wanting the ritual to end, my precious time alone about to end too soon, my own set time but a time set against the world's besieging time. Routine as defence against reality becomes my own self constructed temporary prison cell, repeatedly visited, until made permanent: a place where I go to close the door and lock it from the inside, my precious quiet, my only way of keeping the world at bay. Routine as protection and defence always feels merciful and protective to begin with, while slowly, over time, narrowing our character and our sense of possibility, all the while closing down our freer relationship with time itself.

Routine, as an open doorway to a future life, might actually, at its best, be the ritual of deepening our relationship with time itself, of enriching our appreciation of life and the delightful details and absurdities of everyday existence. Routine can be a way of forming intimate bonds with time itself: through the quiet, meticulous making of our morning coffee or the brewing of our tea; through drinking that welcome brew in the same chair, at the same time, looking out through the very same window, but at a different daily, changing sky, seeing the world move through the seasons and all the while placing ourselves, without moving, without any apparent outside change, in the midst of the eternal and the untrammelled, our seeming unmoving routine, at the frontier of all the changes occurring in our very moveable world.

At its very best, routine is a central pillar of an inquisitive life, a consciously performed ritual, a living, repeated invitation: a way of constantly creating and deepening possibilities, and of actually getting something done over time. Routine that carries the timeless and the exploratory, can become the central foundation of keeping a relationship alive, of writing a book, raising a family, building a house. We make a miracle out of simply turning up, at the same time to do the same good work, watching that work mature, slowly, with our daily visitations, into something we could not fully imagine, before we gave ourselves over to that daily, dedicated, repeated, miraculous act of appearance and disappearance at the waiting desk or at our well-loved familiar workbench.

Routine as mere routine, can also be an empty death spiral. Routine without a living engagement with the timeless and changeable world outside of our necessary daily tasks always turns into dark unconscious magic: it is routine as the casting of repeated spells upon our own senses; to dull them and thus unconsciously lose an edge which has become too sharp and too painful for us to wield. As defences and insulation, our routines become daily incantations meant to damp down our faculties and to keep the world at bay. Routine becomes a ritual mode of defence: the hope being that if we can immobilise our self we can immobilise the unforgiving incomprehensible world around us. The worst and most damaging routines might be the repeated things we say to ourselves about the impossibility of any other life than this life, than this routine, which we then repeat routinely to a bored world, a world which unfortunately, has heard it all before and which is glad to turn away from our cynicism.

Routines, used as cover, over a sustained time can kill our creativity: the immediate morning refuge in our screens an addictive invitation to doom-scroll through news that carries nothing except the corroboration of our hopelessness, looking endlessly for messages that in the end carry nothing of what we really wish to hear. Routines can become a way of locking ourselves in place, the addiction to continually breaking news, the loss of anticipation for our own inner revelations, the forlorn hope for some kind of outside force that will have the strength and power to break through our inner deadlock. Routines need our attention and our observation, routines can be a matter of life and death.

Routines that are life giving, routines as living engagement only look like routines from the outside: a settled creative routine may only look like the unchanging, boring every day existence we love to condemn: but everything in a fully engaged creative ritual of routine is being invisibly cradled into life inside that still figure shaving maple at the workbench, or the silhouette chopping onions against the kitchen window, or the seated practitioner, sitting stock still against the wall, unmoving on the black meditation mat.

But every routine, no matter how creatively engaged to begin with, no matter how much it was or is a good servant to our completing a certain task, always becomes in the end a barrier to our becoming, a way of forgetting and a cloud of unknowing amnesia. Routines have a life span, a seasonality, a place and a time in our lives: routines are not meant to go on routinely, forever. Routines in the longer wave form of a human life are unrepeatable. A proper, creative, nourishing routine takes real imagination and real adaptability to sustain. Routine is anything but routine: routine is the central, ever changing discipline of an evolving, maturing, creative and ever surprising life.

SEX

is a word that deserves our deepest sympathy. Sex is a word that has never been able to do its job properly, because it never had a chance of carrying the meaning we ask of it. Sex is a poor, put-upon word that has been asked to carry on its too short back, in its single brief, appropriately flattening syllable, something it was never qualified to hold and something it was never qualified to explain. Sex is a salacious word exactly because it veils what it means, and simultaneously promises far more than it can ever deliver.

Sex is a word we use to describe something we have actually become afraid of understanding and therefore want to abstract into a false form of knowledge, hence, the falsity of the word. We mention that two people had sex as if we know what actually might have happened between them, when in actual fact the couple in question rarely know what happened to them, either individually or as a temporary duo. What actually happened is calibrated by the presence or absence of incalculable physical and imaginative chemistry. Sex is how we describe something from the outside in; a word we use when we become afraid of investigating the very origins of attraction and passion itself, when we are afraid of carrying from our deeper and darker unspoken sources, the truer understandings that might transform our outer, light-filled world.

Sex is a word that should be retired so that it can rise again in another guise, its short flat vowel sound replaced by calling on a deeper, life-like range of language equal to the broad sensual spectrum of experiences we are trying to invoke. The very use of the word sex means we have missed the point; no single word should be asked to carry the orchestral bodily ache, magnified by the imagination, spurred by the almost religious invitation, consummated by an astonishing physical melding, or by our hopes for a truer meeting with another or with ourselves: when we wish to disappear physically and psychologically, totally and completely in the astonishing oblivion of orgasm or near orgasm. The word only really describes what we experience in the absence of any of the above.

Sex as a word should be given a long holiday from our mouths and from our societies for the next hundred and fifty years, to make up for its terrible misuse in narrowing our minds over the last hundred and fifty years; it is a word that should be given back to its original use of scientific and sexual classification, so that we can look back on the quaint, narrow attempt on the part of the last few generations to solidify in one word, something that actually carries the timeless tidal nature of life itself.

Sex is a prose word masking what only the volcanic vocabulary of poetry can describe. What is longing to be described in its literal eruptions and freeing, unrestrained wildness are words that carry the tidal fluidity of life, and that are equal to the overwhelming powers of sexuality and sensuality itself. The single word sex, like a lid on our understanding, hides what it is meant to uncover: half of what lies in our sexual nature is taboo and always will be taboo to our human societies fighting against the constantly threatening and engulfing forces of life and death: what lies powerfully, broodingly, dormant beneath the word sex is not amenable to the easy explanations of a single word. Sex is an isolating word, its brief annunciation unconsciously meant to insulate us from understanding and facing the overwhelming power of life wishing to create life itself, where our individual happiness is just a drop in the ocean of ongoing existence, a vain attempt to be constantly self-asserting, self-understanding and self-defining.

Sex is the word used by the part of the mind cut off from bodily experience: the body that actually experiences its true nature is a double doorway that leads both ways into life and death. Strangely, through the tiny deaths experienced in sensually meeting another we literally bring life into the world: what lies behind the word sex is our early and repeated reconnaissance into the experience and disappearances of our own eventual death.

Sex is the word we use to describe our unconscious wish for boundaries and defences against the unbounded and the ultimately un-understandable: the wish to keep at bay in a simple word those constant seasonal powers that outline our own powerlessness against the eternal, tidal, violations of our sense of self that the boundary-less, tidal nature of the world constantly inflicts. Sex is the poor over-short, over-burdened word that has to carry the entire spectrum of human sensuality and human identity in all its appearances and disappearances, through all our pains and in all our ecstatic sorrows.

The word needs our help, and should have our sympathy when we hear it, but we should know that when we do hear the word, we are hearing a word, that almost always, by itself, and despite all the fuss, means next to nothing.

SHAME

is nothing to be shameful about. Shame is the very physical, heartrending, painful measure of the way we hide from life and from others because we do not feel equal to the astonishing nature of what we meet. Shame calibrates all the ways, great and small, that we don't measure up: and therefore shame secretly affects even the outwardly shameless and is the core human driver of all human maturation.

Shame outlines exactly the ways we feel inadequate and unequal to life and exactly the nature and place of our hiding. Shame provides us, generously and on a daily basis, with the invitation to understand all the ways we do not wish or do not deserve to be seen, to be touched or to be invited to join the extraordinary dance of the world: shame tells us instantly all the ways we desire to meet but dare not meet, all the ways we are desperate to play but do not play; all the ways we desire to sing but do not sing. Shame tells us all the ways we long for real change but do not feel worthy of the transformation that change brings, and all the ways we deeply desire to be enlivened or to feel pleasure in the extraordinary miracle nature of creation. Shame instructs us in all the ways we feel we do not deserve to be here.

Shame is the interior blind we have drawn over our unexplored, interior nature, or that has been drawn over us by others, in our childhood, in our growing, to keep the blessed, transformative nature of the world at bay. Shame carried unconsciously for a long time or left unexamined becomes the daily unspoken dynamic of undermining ourselves and then in protection of that broken down, undermined identity, trying to prove that everyone and all the world is also undeserving of whatever it thinks deserves.

Shame is the inverse measure of our ability to incarnate fully into our bodies and the vast overwhelming, and astonishing, tidal body of the world.

Shame thrives in secrecy and hiding, shame leads us into dark corners, shame seems not to like to show its face, but therefore in that hiding, we learn to know what we are fearful of, what we are afraid of showing, what we keep from the world: we learn self-compassion. Shame tells us that the nature of our hiding is also a very real gravitational pull toward what we are hiding from: the pull out of that darkness into the light of being seen and being known at some essential, foundational level.

We learn the precise particularities of our well-practised, undeserving natures in the equally precise ways we hide or pretend we have not heard, when we turn up but do not really appear, when we act as if we have not been invited out into the visible by a charismatic other: by a person we deeply desire, by a voice we hear calling us on; that we also wish we could find issuing from our own bodies.

Intense evolutionary pressures and the paramount survival of the tribe mean that our very personal sense of not being seen to measure up is often used against us by the community, by our colleagues, by our societies to keep us in line, to make us feel bad about ourselves; to make us feel physically as if we could 'die of shame' - something that has a powerful, evolutionary, dynamic of communal survival behind it, and something that, in the face of communal survival, it takes tremendous, individual self knowledge to withstand. Being able to examine and find out where we are actually guilty and need to reform, where we need to contribute more, and where we have simply become a scapegoat, is one of our great necessities faced with inherited, societal shame.

Shame entices and invites: in a strange way, shame shamed me and instructed me to write this essay at last, after a long apprenticeship of delay, thinking I was not equal to the task, thinking I had nothing to say on the subject. Shame was my hidden instructor. Shame taught me all the ways I did not feel I was equal to the task. Understanding all the ways I felt I was not equal to the task opened up the sweet territory of my own reluctance for exploration. On finishing this essay I said, 'I have worked all day with shame', and then, with a rueful smile I said to myself: 'you have worked every day of your productive life with shame.'

The particular nature of our shame tells us exactly all the ways we need to come out of hiding. Shame is difficult, shame is painful, shame is our reinforced recoil from the same experiences that previously seemed to break our hearts and made us feel shameful in the first place, but shame is our constant companion, who for our own good and for the sake of our emancipation from all our previous difficulties, will never leave our side. Shame is our faithful and ever-present and ever-helpful friend, inviting us to understand, against all our meticulously gathered evidence, that we deserve to fulfil the desires that often lie unsuspecting and unfelt in the very marrow of our bones.

We should not be ashamed of shame, only perhaps of our reluctance to follow its close, abiding and generous wish to instruct us so carefully in all the ways we feel we have given up on, or are not equal to, the eternal, not-to-be-given-up-on task of living.

SLEEP

is a word that sounds so much like the state itself that just to say the word is an invitation to our own constant, unconscious need for regenerative rest, to fall into depths where we are made new again. The word sleep is almost always said as an imperative: to a child, to someone not well who surely needs it, or half bemused, as we fall unconsciously into its arms, to ourselves, the moment before it happens.

Sleep is not an absence from our onward lives: sleep, our present scientific minds tell us, as our ancient imaginative minds have always told us, is another parallel life, a life constantly attempting to join fully with our waking life in order to make it whole, spacious and even generous to others. Our life asleep, we are surprised to find is just as necessary, has just as much agency and steers our future as much as the one we inhabit while we are awake. Disturbingly and inspiringly, a sleeping life is a life that might be just as 'real' as the life we lead with open eyes.

Sleep is not just a needed support: a foundation to our waking hours, a witnessing, a regeneration and a guiding lodestone to our conscious thoughts: sleep is the invisible parallel life where we grow and mature and learn as much and sometimes more than we do in the busy hours of our lighted days. The quality and depth of our sleep influences our future fate and our destiny as an individual as much as our attempt to make meaning, in our waking, unrested endeavours.

Sleep is not just a necessary: sleep is the nested hidden driver of our onward maturation. We might stop complaining that we spend half of our life asleep and face up to the real dynamic that often, in this waking life, we only seem to be paying real attention, and that our sleeping self is in its own beautifully contradictory fashion, actually the life that is constantly trying to bring us awake to what is really occurring both around us and within us.

The foundation of any fully awake conscious life, sleep resides in the essence of every living thing and was with us before we developed consciousness or even a nervous system that could create consciousness. Sleep is as ancient as life itself, and lives in the very cellular nature of our identity. Our planktonic evolutionary ancestors rose and fell through dream-like columns of the ocean, their little cilia beating them up to the surface until the light in the broad, uninhabited sky above began to fade into the unseen evening, causing them to produce the selfsame melatonin we produce to this day: inhibiting the rhythmic beat of their tiny limbs and having them fall, as we seem to too, into sleep, through the darker layers of reality, and then once more, to 'rise' again as we do with the morning light.

Sleep is protective: the guardian, not only of our safety, but of our care for others: without sleep not only do we become exhausted but everyone and everything becomes exhausting: with a rested sleep we broaden and deepen our sense of spaciousness; our ability to be patient, to listen, to reach out and help another.

Sleep is instructive in the way it opens us up as much as closes us down, the thalamus, that astonishing nexus of cells nesting at the protected centre of the brain that creates our sense of being a conscious, attentive, separateness - in other words, gives us a sense of self - 'closes down' in sleep, not by ceasing to function or drawing a veil over its activities, but by producing rhythmic bursts of neuronic activity that overwhelm the inward coming stimulus of the eyes, the ears or the reactive peripheral mind.

Interestingly, the task of the thalamus, the central biological foundation of our identity, is to govern sleep as actively as it governs alertness.

Breath is intimately connected to the ability to sleep: we cannot actively will ourselves to sleep, we can only give ourselves over to the breath that will naturally carry us there. Emerging from unrested sleep, studies tell us that the tired mind remembers negative experiences and holds on to the worst interpretations of that experience: the rested, well-slept mind and body strives for context and ultimately forgiveness. Without true rest and disappearance, all outward appearances become interferences and sources of irritation. When our eyes are tired the world seems tired also. When our vision has gone; it seems as if no part of the world can find us.

The rest and regeneration we find in sleep calls for as much discipline and preparedness as our so called conscious mind; but it is a discipline that calls for undoing and letting go rather than doing and holding on: undoing the need to worry, undoing the need to be counting and comparing constantly, to hold on too tightly, to control and be anxious. To give ourselves over to sleep we do not strive toward that goal - to give ourselves to sleep we actually give ourselves over to the breath, we learn to 'fall' asleep - to fall, as we should learn to fall in our waking lives, to another deeper foundation of rested understanding, that can re-imagine all our goals. In sleep we learn to descend, to a previously unvisited centre where the seemingly uncontrollable dynamics and threats of existence suddenly constellate into recognisable patterns; patterns that seem to be re-woven, simply by seeing them from a rested centre.

Our sleeping self is often more grounded in reality, more aware of the real sense of our health, psychological and physical, than our waking self. It has a truer sense of the body's exhaustion, tiredness or underlying anxieties than the person often just trying to catch up with itself while awake.

Waking from a good sleep we often see to our astonishment that we ourselves manufactured and authored many of the threats and difficulties that kept us awake the night before; that the invitational undoing at the centre of sleep has granted us, a certain wild freedom, perspective and mercy.

Sleep is mercy itself: even in our nightmares we are being told in no uncertain terms that we are living the lighted hours in the wrong way: that something must be attended to, changed and almost always, healed. Good sleep is not only where the best advice is heard but often dramatically and decisively demonstrated.

The answer we wake with from profound rest is almost always both freeing and relational. Restorative sleep at its best always brings us to a radical form of simplification: the simple, healing word of apology or the transformative act of making an invitation that should have been made long ago. The willingness to see, from a deeper perspective and as if for the first time, in the rising of the sun and the coming of the morning, the miraculous nature and intimate otherness of the world.

The invisible hours of the night are where we harvest and understand what we have taken so much effort in the day to sow and grow. The visible hours of the day are where we harvest what we have unconsciously taken so much effort in the invisible hours of the night to re-imagine. When we deepen the friendship between sleep and wakefulness we magnify both inner and outer forms of presence to make one presence, holding the visible and the invisible together, each reinforcing one other. Falling fast asleep on our pillows, or coming back to this world in the dawn light from what only seems like another world, we pause at that astonishing boundary between sleep and wakefulness, and in the rising of the sun and the coming of the morning, we have the possibility of experiencing in the shift from one to another, the sheer miraculous otherness and intimate togetherness of our inner and outer worlds.

SOJOURN

is what we all do, every day of our restless lives: arrive, stay a while and then move on. Sojourn captures that simultaneous sense of recent arrival, intriguing stay, and adventurous departure necessary to the underlying joy and happiness of our human essence. Sojourn is a word that melds the three tenses of past, present and future together. We are creatures of the sudden hello, the getting to know and the long or the short goodbye, but sojourn is also a word that understands that even in our briefest stays we are changing and being changed by what we stay with. Staying with something is to change and deepen whatever we are staying with; staying itself is a journey that always leads to altering our further departures. Sojourn takes its definition by being a stay between journeys that is also a journey in itself.

Human beings love the idea and the ideal of the eternal and the unchanging, but seem to meet that eternal only in the never ending invitation to see and experience the underlying, unstoppable, changing nature of existence. We intuitively understand that we conspire in this state of affairs, we are both helpless witnesses and unconscious engines of change every moment of our day, witnessing and causing trouble even in our simple passing through. Indeed, there is no trouble-making change agent to match our very own body, which moves on without our asking or without a bye or leave, through the thresholds of maturation, without a stop or a halt. By the agency of some hidden, unstoppable driver of change, the body makes its pilgrim way through childhood, into adolescence, into adulthood, into eldership, into the sudden realisation that our next journey is into our own disappearance, all accompanied we hope, by our own noble attempt at a brave goodbye. The body we realise, seeing in that one single glance in the mirror, the youth we were, the person we are now and the elder we are about to become, is the ultimate sojourner.

Whether we are world travellers or home loving stick-in-the-muds, we are creatures always just traveling through: our essence and our attention caught, even as we sit reading in our arm chairs, or gaze at our screens, by mythological images that mirror our traveling nature: that stranger at the door asking for alms and hospitality, that handsome traveller at a bar asking not so innocently for a good time, that good Samaritan on the road offering to help, that ultimate pilgrim of the restless, Clint Eastwood, turning his horse toward the sunset, having freed the town from awful predators, all of us, believers or not, vicarious travellers in great and timeless religious images inherited from our past: Christ entering Jerusalem, St Paul struck down on the road to Damascus, Basho's narrow road to the deep north; all of us, caught imaginatively whether we go or not, by the pilgrim roads of the world: the road to Varanasi, the road to Santiago, the road to Graceland, the trackless roads across the oceans our ancestors explored: all beckoning us on to some place where something wonderful already happened and where something wonderful, something beyond my present, might well happen to me.

The underlying undertow of existence, even in our most rested state is restless, tidal change, and our agency and context for this restless travel is longing in all its forms: physiological and psychological: even Zen students, refusing to move, sitting stock still in their black robes on their black cushions travel invisibly on the road of longing: the longing, strangely, to be free of the restless mind, in order to be at rest with the true, underlying restless movement of the world. Each of us, sojourners all, even when we seem to be as quiet and as still as a mouse, journeying on into some other, longed for spaciousness, every step of our restless way.

STOPPING

is how we go on. Stopping is how we deepen our relationship with the world and those who live in it. Stopping is how we drink from a more nourishing source. Stopping is both illusory and absolutely necessary and calls for a deep, silent, bodily attention to understand what is being brought to a halt and therefore what is continuing to move and grow despite everything we do. Stopping is the essence of change and the signature of an evolving and vital life: the invitation to re-understand the essence of what needs to be brought to a halt, in order to proceed at a deeper level.

Stopping involves identifying what needs to be given up, but the dynamic of stopping also identifies what cannot be stopped at every crucial threshold in a human life. Identifying what needs to be stopped and what cannot be stopped, is foundational to our moving on in a better way. Human beings always need to cease doing things when something better can emerge. Human beings always need to join and help to transform, what cannot be stopped.

Stopping is the foundational necessity for our own sense of personal freedom and the ability to choose our future.

In halting something that is neither good for me nor the world I feel the essence of personal freedom, and the sense that, on the other side of what is being stopped, there might be a better way. Stopping is the first step human beings take in deepening and moving on, in any necessary, crucial conversation.

Stopping is illusory: nothing really ever stops, what we recognise as stopping is the sudden immobilisation of the surface while the essence flows on, underneath and often despite the surface. But surfaces are also what human beings first meet, understand and then cling to in their lives and so stopping is found everywhere as a heartbreaking and necessary part of our lives: at work, at home or in the far reaches of the natural world.

The heart-stopping dynamic of things just suddenly stopping surrounds us and informs us in every emerging, constellating aspect of the created world. Stopping can feel like dying, because it is, so often, in fact, dying, the passing of friends and loved ones, but also dying to be reborn. Like dying, stopping can feel like a breakdown of our identity. The breath stopping is how life is ended, but stopping is also the dynamic from which the new, the astonishing and the often overwhelming emerges: playful tiger kittens stop being playful and turn into stalking, dangerous, predatory adults; small, atmospheric, desultory disturbances over equatorial waters stop being unrecognisable and organise into vast hurricanes sweeping over Florida; and then thankfully, hurricanes stop being hurricanes, blowing themselves out over calmer inland territories that absorb their previously fierce embrace.

Wherever we look, we find things stopping in every domestic domain of a human life; looking out of our kitchen window, spring stops being spring to turn into summer; tight buds stop being tight buds to unfurl into luxuriant leaves, and luxuriant leaves fall from trees to create the necessary, survivable, silhouettes of winter.

The entire spectrum of human existence is involved with stopping: the kettle clicks off at boiling point signalling a time for tea or coffee; the heart monitor flat lines signalling the time for saying goodbye; stopping is simultaneously our greatest mercy and our necessary grief and so often cuts us to the quick: products we have spent years bringing to market stop being wanted; homes suddenly stop being homes and become heavy burdens we are forced to carry - happy marriages stop being happy marriages and become difficult memories - collaborative workplaces turn into dictatorial domains, and the human frame one fine day and against our will, suddenly seems to be about to stop breathing. Stopping, seen fully is often the measure of our fear of death and the constant reminder of our coming mortality. Stopping asks us to make our relationship to time and the time that we have more intimate.

Stopping is almost always something we initially do not want but have to learn in order to mature: as in stopping saying certain things to ourselves, or to others; as in stopping drinking, stopping smoking, stopping eating too much: or even stopping trying to give things up: anything that tries to hold its original form through the changing circumstances of a life or of the changing necessities of own maturing bodies, will not survive in any vital form. Anything that cannot stop being its inherited self at least temporarily is actually contributing to its own disappearance or demise: the young wine connoisseur with a vast collection suddenly finds in later life that they now possess a stomach that rebels against even the merest sip of red wine; the car collector now finds all the constant maintenance nothing but a bother, the homebody out of nowhere suddenly hankers for the freedom of the road. Every business leader at one time or another, finds their previous understanding of success, the very thing that prevents anything new and innovative from happening.

Stopping is necessary; stopping is never ending. Stopping, we realise if we want to be participants in this never ending, ever present, ever inviting dynamic, actually needs to be taken on as an art and a practice. The act and the art of stopping, the art and act of asking what needs to be stopped, and the art of learning how to stop things before it is too late, will always be my first step in deepening the conversation.

Stopping is only possible by having a friendship with silence. The unhealthy conversation, in a marriage, in a workplace in a deeply personal life, is always achieved by the entrance into a bodily, observational silence. Without silence I simply find my mind describing and judging everything in the same old familiar way, without silence I stop nothing. Without silence I become afraid of seeing what needs to be stopped. Without silence I stop stopping things. Without silence I cannot courageously bring the outer exchange to a halt in order to re-imagine it at the centre.

To stop an unhealthy, immobilising conversation is not to re-engineer it, not to come at it a different way, is not to make a course correction - no, it is actually to cease it all together and begin a silent, attentive, observational conversation with the unknown that lies within me and beyond me. What I have described as the enemy of my aims is never the true enemy of my aims, the enemy of my deeper aim in life is my own inability to bring the surface conversation to a halt and hold the conversation at a deeper level and, in silence.

Stopping is actually dropping: dropping down to a deeper level closer to the pivot point from which the surrounding complexity of my life originates and takes form. Stopping is dropping down to a place of real movement. From this deeper pivot point I begin to see not only the way things can be moved, but all the ways I have refused to move myself, and therefore contributed to my previous immobility.

Stopping occurs unconsciously through exhaustion, when we do not know how to do it any other way, but we can stop things consciously when we stay close to our need for rest. When we feel a lack of nourishment from our life at the surface, or our surface work or our surface relationship, and a thirst for another deeper life, we learn to stop the conversation at the surface at increasingly earlier stages of the unproductive cycle, we stop the exchange, not to retreat from life or work or relationship - but to stay closer to the centre - to drink, so to speak, from a deeper well.

Stopping a conversation, a relationship, a direction in a workplace is often the most courageous act we can take in our lives. As time goes by, we learn to stop conversations that are imprisoning us by the very way we are holding that conversation. We move on simply by talking about things in a better, more nourishing, more foundational way.

We learn the art and practice of stopping so that we can join a deeper, onward moving, unstoppable tide; one we have always intuited to lie beneath everything that seems immoveable in our lives. The radical act of stopping things is actually the radical act of moving on in a better way, always to begin with - invisibly, always to begin with toward the unknown - and almost always, slightly to our grief, bringing our previous forms of happiness to a halt in order to move on toward a greater future happiness, always living; always waiting, just beyond our present understanding.

STUMBLE

is a word that carries the bump of coming to earth deep within that very first, arresting vowel sound, setting a brake to our forward motion and setting a limit to our sense of being forever well balanced, in control and always on our successful way.

Stumble rightly carries the same echoing sound and the same echoing reminder as the word humble and the same import as its cousin, humility, which derives from humus, which is the substance to which we are returned, both when we stumble and when we are returned, in our final falling, to the very earth that gave us our foundation. To stumble is to return to the ground on which we have been walking all along and signals the involuntary point in our lives where we unconsciously needed to return to it, stumbling highlights exactly the way in which we have not been paying attention. Sometimes we stumble just to find that underlying ground again for reassurance, sometimes to be able to step off from that ground in a better and firmer way, sometimes just to get the earth beneath our finger nails again or to feel the body as a body again, even if it is only through a bruise on our knees or the sharp, stinging reminder of a barked shin.

A stumble is often seen as a mistake or an accident, but a stumble is, in effect, something that has always been waiting for us all along, arresting us when we get above ourselves, making us look again when we have stopped paying attention, having us be aware when we were pushed on purpose, or even more soberly, reminding us of our mortality when we get to an age where our legs won't carry us anymore. Given our propensity for getting above ourselves, for not paying attention, for making enemies and for ageing despite all our best efforts, stumbling is just a matter of time. Stumbling brings us into this time and this very moment and this very threshold of our maturation. The stumble we have just taken has been waiting to instruct us all along, mostly in all the ways we are absent, not quite here, or haven't been paying attention.

No matter how successful we have been in the past, or how admired we are by others in the present, no matter how well we comport ourselves through the generality of our days, there are times and epochs where the only way we are allowed to endure a particular day and get through that day, is by tripping and stumbling through its morning, floundering through its long afternoon and losing our footing on the stairs at the end of a hopefully brief evening. Stumble is surprise: I did not know I would stumble until I did: debilitation always arrives, almost by definition, from an unlooked direction - my success on the stock market guarantees no immunity from the blows of emotional loss - my success in creating a calm, mindful state offers no defences against financial disaster: we mere mortals are overwhelmed by circumstance no matter the path we take or make through life and all of us experience that abiding, inevitable stumble of being fit and healthy until the sudden, sobering, fateful day we come to realise we are not.

Stumbling is an essential part of our human journey; some kind of instructive stumble is waiting for us now and lies just around the very next corner of our lives: sometimes, stumbling is actually essential and necessary: many of the experiences in which we gain compassion for others, can only be earned by limping painfully through them or at times crossing the necessary line of earned experience by crawling on our hands and knees, so that we can come to understand perhaps, in our very bones, just how much of humanity is already on its hands and knees every day of the ycar.

We hope not to stumble, we try not to stumble, we watch our feet and we watch the path upon which we place our feet, but all of us know it is just a matter of time: better then to help those around us who are stumbling now while we are still upright, better to know that sometimes the next perspective will come from looking up from a very low elevation at someone reaching down to offer a helping hand. None of us is exempt from a fall, none of us is immune from a stumble, in public or in secret. Stumbling is just a consciously, unconscious way of stopping so that we can try to start again in a better way.

Buddha was once asked by a very honest man what he should do about the fact that although he felt incredibly virtuous whenever he was actually listening to Buddha teach, he would almost immediately go straight off drinking, carousing and generally making a fool of himself, waking up the very next day, with a bad hangover, having literally fallen down somewhere at the roadside. The question was: 'What should he do about stumbling and falling down every day from the high standard of the teachings?' Buddha answered that the solution was very simple. 'When you fall, or when you stumble, just make sure you stumble in the very direction in which you wish to go.'

THE

is not as definite an article as it sounds. The word *the* isolates and exiles whatever it outlines from any proper context with anything else, the word *the* attempts definition without context but the only true definition of anything might be one that places it in a larger context, and every context is a moving, changeable story that moves and changes according to how vital we make it, or the living depth to which we understand it. *The* is our attempt to lasso reality, eliminate its larger context and then bring it to an illusory ground that will allow us to believe we understand what we are describing. The word *the* is definitely not the most definite article, describing reality, we would like it to be.

The person we are speaking of is not the person we imagine, *the* sound of rain falling is far more than moisture and patter of drops on a tin roof, *the* understanding I previously had will be proved just as illusory as the one I have now. *The* relationship I think I am in is most definitely not the relationship I am actually experiencing. *The* context I have arranged for myself at present will always be made absurd by the greater context which I am just coming to understand. '*The* thing is', as a way of beginning a sentence that carries our definite opinion, will not admit that the thing we think, might not be *the* thing at all. *The* cat is not the essence of the cat, *the* cat is actually a mystery, as is the mat it sits on. The word *the* only ignores a larger mystery; in fact, it is such a distraction that many languages do without it altogether.

Japanese, Chinese, Estonian and Finnish are just some of many languages that refuse to commit themselves to the illusionary definite article. It might be no accident that the Zen tradition, nurtured most fully in China and Japan, has always been rightly sceptical of all the ways we try to define things far ahead of actually understanding them; all the ways we attempt to announce their names too definitely, and most especially through the word *the*. Zen and all the contemplative traditions of the world that share the approach of deep silent attention always ask us to lessen or eliminate our language's discriminating, mediating and sabotaging effects on our perceptions.

The word *the* is our ever-present, almost invisible, false friend and probably one of the main culprits in the way we sabotage our intimacy with things other than ourselves, hiding itself as a word, innocuously, in plain sight, helping our carefully constructed illusions almost insidiously, in every sentence.

The rain in Spain does not fall mainly on *the* plain; the rain in Spain has never fallen mainly on the plain. *The* rain and *the* plain and everything that is not rain or a plain are a multiplicity and a moveable essence far beyond our understanding, they are actually the real article, one that can never be reduced to a single, definite, illusory article.

The word *the* is an overestimation of our powers.

TIME

is on our side, time is not our enemy, time is our greatest friend. If we can come to know time in its own intimate, unfolding way and not through the abstract measure we have made of it, time starts to grant a greater, more spacious, more elemental and even eternal freedom to every mortal, seemingly time-bound human life.

Time is not slipping through our fingers, time is here forever, it is we who are slipping through the fingers of time. Memory and the traces of memory grant me a sense of time passing and also enable me to learn. How I remember through time and how I learn and how I put those memories and that learning into conversation with the future shapes my identity for good or for ill.

Time is at the centre of my identity. Time only seems to be something in which I participate involuntarily, but time needs me voluntarily to deepen my understanding of its multivalent nature and help to mediate its life fully in my world. Time needs me: needs me to live through all its many appearances, to give it life and amplitude. Time exists in a field of possibility which I influence and partly determine. I may constantly cry that I need more time, but actually time needs more of me - more of our spacious, uninterrupted timeless time to live out and understand both its extraordinary depths and its incalculable far off horizons.

Time teaches us that nothing at the surface is as it seems, but also, that all the surface seemings of the world depend upon the all embracing multi-level, presence of time. Nothing could happen and nothing could be remembered in our lives were it not for that strange multi-dimensional, multi-level quality we reduce to calling time: not the functioning of a single human cell, the vast weather systems passing through our skies nor the surrounding cosmos of our planetary systems. Time is both the ground beneath our feet and the spacious sky under which everything is allowed to happen.

Time may take a linear form in my mind but only because my senses are narrow: my mind given to defensive postures; to surfaces and unimaginative forms that restrict my understanding of the multi-dimensional, radiant nature of existence. Time not only invites me below all surfaces but in all directions at once, including, frighteningly, when time seemingly turns back toward me and looks me in the face. Time may seem always to be flowing away from me but in deeper states of attention I and time are reciprocal partners in crime, we create a multi-faceted, conversational reality together, not only through memory but through direct experience. Seeing the multitudinous face of time itself and courageously holding its gaze is one of the great thresholds of religious transformation.

When my sense of time breaks out of the linear so does my identity. In the deeper, timeless states of love or newly being in love, time radiates out from the very place where I am standing, unbinding me from the well fitted, previously time-bound manacles of my routine life. The sudden freedom felt when time is opened by the power of love always makes me click my heels.

The entrance into time is always the threshold where we are asked to loosen our grasp on our previous, fearful understandings. Love is time unanchored and let to be fully itself where the hours are rich and spacious with anticipation and the sudden sense that there is no immediate horizon to our possibilities.

Without love, and the all round attention love pays to the world, time is where I feel most powerless, because time passes and I will die, so I hold on, of course, to a version of time mediated through control, exhausting my very power to live through the very force of my grip. Living fully and giving freedom to those who live with me, often means letting go of the way I hold onto time, and all the ways I hold on to the people I love too strictly, too narrowly and too unimaginatively to my particular version of time.

Whatever the version of time we have arranged for ourselves, time always feels like a powerful gravity: a pull to our senses; always drawing us toward a clock, toward an appointment, toward a sense that something should be happening now, whether it is actually possible or not.

Time is intimately connected with gravity. Astonishingly, physicists tell our disbelieving ears that everything gravitates toward places where time moves more slowly, and time seems to move more slowly the greater the mass to which it is near. The greater the gravity, the greater the slowing down of time, so that, to our amazement, someone living on a mountaintop ages more quickly than their neighbours down in the valley. What physicists call mass, we could also call presence, and as in a human life, presence is invitational, presence invites other presences toward it, presence slows time down and opens up possibilities of experiencing the timeless and the eternal. The depth, amplitude and invitational nature of my presence slows time for everyone around me. Timelessness is the foundation of real charism and charisma. By creating a centred, timeless presence, I invite everyone unconsciously to make the choice to join me there or, should they be afraid of what might happen in that slow spacious territory of possibility, run a hundred miles in the opposite direction.

What is disturbing about time in my mortal human world is that my personal surface experience of it is irrevocable: the glass broken into a hundred shards cannot heal itself, the child I lost will never return to me, the regrets I have are things I can only heal in my imagination or with others in my future who might benefit from the sincerity of my regrets. But this arrow of time exists only at the surface of things; when I die, the individual atoms and molecules of my body actually experience, not time passing, but a change of state, a transition from an ordered world to one at another level, newly disordered, but also full of new potential. The meeting of time and the timeless is the place of my inevitable transformation. Time tells me, with some glee, that we are all compost for many future lives and many future worlds.

Time never comes to an end, even though my time will come to an end, time does not pass, even though I will pass, time will carry on to eternity, therefore a proper relationship with the foundational nature of time is my own, everyday doorway into that eternal.

When I stop counting time, as a way of controlling it, I stop my addiction to naming the hours and what should occur in those hours: that single pathway across the field, suddenly branches to a hundred more, no one has explored; that thirty minutes with my son or daughter, fully spent, lives for years as a precious memory. When we stop measuring change as if we knew what measuring change actually meant, the human ability to measure time also stops, which is why, on a silent retreat or in a monastery, we make all the outer hours repeatable so that, day after day, nothing on the outside seems to change: we stop time on the outside so that we can concentrate on the way things change and grow on the inside: we dwell in the deepening, broadening and maturing sense of presence we call the timeless.

As our war against time quietens, we take joy in the increased acuity of the ears: the entrancing aromas of rain on fresh leaves that we previously never gave ourselves the time to breathe: time is left to itself, to be itself, and to grow what it needs to grow in every season of a human life. In a deeply rested state, as we loosen our grip on what we think is time: our sense of bodily tension falls away, along with the falling away of a falsely measured self and out of that we begin to experience that joyful radiance we call timelessness, growing through every cell of our previously time-bound bodies, just like now, as I write these last lines, in the quiet late night hours, in a hotel bar in Italy, listening to miracle hands moving softly over the keys of a perfectly tuned piano: memory meeting the moment in each note and then memory and moment both disappearing and reappearing in the onward music, each note exquisitely timed, but part of an onward unstoppable flow, this moment in time, inherited from all previous times, rippling into the future - for all time.

UNDECEIVED

is a word magnified to the tenth power by the word that lives right at its heart: to become undeceived is to find, often suddenly and traumatically, a precious sense of freedom hidden by the very way we were deceived in the first place. Being undeceived is almost always accompanied by the revelation that we had the evidence all along, that not only were we unconsciously aware we were being deceived but for the sake of some deeper psychological goal, hidden by our surface minds, we were actually willing and active participants in exactly the way we were deeply misled. To become undeceived is to become unbound, not only from the prison of the past, but from the very identity we inhabited to shape our part in the deception.

To become undeceived is to realise we were deceived, not only by a set of given circumstances: a fraudster on the phone, an over-promising investment, a manipulating lover, but by our own self-sabotaging goals, goals that were then easily used to manipulate us, to play upon us, to trap us.

The word undeceived always carries a sense of surveying our past, as if admitting that most of the time human beings live with some form of collective deception or, individually, have been deceiving themselves for longer than they would like to admit. All paths to freedom and enlightenment in our ancient, contemplative traditions work on the dynamic of becoming undeceived, of breaking through illusion and seeing to the heart of things and most practically, seeing to the heart of things by bringing three powerful dynamics together: attention, silence and the breath. We begin the practice of becoming undeceived by paying attention in ever deepening silence while following the natural rhythm of the breath.

Our willingness to be deceived can many times be measured by our distance from the revelations of attentive silence and the natural rhythms of give and take we find in the body and the breath. Often we are being manipulated or are willing to manipulate, because we have literally become afraid of breathing out properly and have shaped an identity that is always breathing in, always, in a way, physically and metaphorically, taking too much, too much of the time. To give and receive, as instructed by the natural rhythm of the breath in the body and in a proper rhythmic seasonal manner, is to be released from the unceasing goals that warp our characters and make them susceptible to the self deceptions that double as our armour and our protections.

The willingness to be undeceived is always difficult because it is almost always the willingness to be humiliated: the measure of our humility is the measure of our wish to be undeceived; to admit to the way we have been fooling ourselves, to come to terms with our own inadequate hearing, our blindness, and our unwillingness to look beneath the surface of a world we did not wish to disturb. To become undeceived is to let go, most especially at our last breath, of all the elaborate strategies we have employed to stay away from the truth.

The measure of our humility is the measure of our wish to be undeceived. The moment we are undeceived is the moment we realise we were deceived all along, that we did not understand, that we were led astray or that we trusted a person or a path that should not have been trusted: to be undeceived is to be released from the prison of our misconception. The word *deceive* in Latin meant to become entrapped; to be undeceived is to be released from the prison of our false understanding.

The measure of our maturity as a human being is the measure of our willingness to be undeceived on a moment by moment basis: by evidence, by paying attention, by listening to what we are told; by realising how much of what we have been telling ourselves has been a nonsense all along.

Being undeceived calls for self-compassion and self-forgiveness in letting go of the way we wanted things to be, and most importantly in understanding that deception is part of the warp and weft of creation. The word *undeceived*'s unusual inversion of the more commonly used *deceived* tells us just how much deception is more common than perception. Deception is a necessary part of existence, from the biological imperatives of camouflage and mimicry, of one thing looking like another, to the way we are deceived on a daily basis by the false promises inherent in what we buy and consume, by the half-truths adults tell us to protect us as children from the fiercer aspects of our world; by the self deception necessary to hide from ourselves the future consequences of our own present bravery. Self-deception, in fact, may be an act of self-compassion, holding us back from the full understanding of what is going on until we are ready to face it, ready to change and ready for the new life it entails.

To be undeceived not only tells us that we have understood something, but that we have been willing and humble enough to admit that previously we were held, were imprisoned by, were shaped by, and even held others hostage to, the opposite.

The word undeceived is powerful and decisive, because all of us intuit that no matter how long we have been deceived, we are, in this very moment, if we pay real attention, being given the opportunity to stand on the very threshold, the dizzy precipice, the very cliff face, of being undeceived.

UNHAPPINESS

is divine discontent. Unhappiness is how we get to a better, happier place. Unhappiness is revelation: unhappiness fully understood is a physical, emotional and intellectual breakthrough that tells us that for now, we are in the wrong place, living with the wrong person or even, to our continued exasperation, shaping the wrong kind of life or the wrong kind of body.

The invitation to understand our unhappiness takes many subtle forms: we may be doing the right work at the right place but doing it in all the wrong ways, we may be unhappy because of something we know but haven't yet come to terms with, or something that we do not know that we wish we did. Unhappiness is our beautiful instructor in recognising and pointing out the intuitively wrong and the visibly not quite right. Unhappiness is our constant companion: that difficult friend who continually insists on telling us the truth for our own good. Unhappiness is on our side.

Unhappiness takes me down, because down is where I need to go, to the ground of a new understanding, to the place, underneath all the surface discontent, where I will understand exactly why I am not happy; exactly what I am missing in my life and what particular form of courage I will need in my wish to live a better, happier life.

Unhappiness asks not to flee its presence but to pay a very sharp attention to all its various forms and the way they come to live in our bodies and our lives. Unhappiness is more like a flow of experience, a river of ups and downs becoming deep stationary pools, then moving on again, than a solid immoveable lump: unhappiness asks us to follow those flows to their origin; to the very deepest pool it forms in our bodies and our minds, so that as we enter and descend into its depths, we might trace it to its source.

Unhappiness is not only our pointer toward things that are bad for our sense of wellbeing, but it also leads us to those sources where we start to understand how much we continually substitute false, abstract conversations for real experience and even more importantly, the way these substitutions tell us all the ways we feel we don't deserve to drink from the very physical sources that can actually create real joy.

Unhappiness asks us to say no, more clearly, more often and more emphatically to all the things we experience in the sphere of my unhappiness that have made me smaller, less generous and less present. Discontent, observed and transformed may be a better pathway to maturity than a too-protected contentment. Unhappiness is an edge that followed closely and sincerely can become my leading edge.

Unhappiness is the first step in the rehabilitation of longing in our lives; in deep unhappiness and melancholy we experience an absolute physical sense, not only of what is missing in our lives, but how much resistance we continually exert in finding out what is missing. Unhappiness measures the distance from what I want.

A state of seemingly permanent unhappiness is often the permanent state of refusing to feel the deeper underlying grief, living untouched underneath our exterior life - an underlying grief that cannot be ignored and that our unhappiness is trying to have us properly visit and understand. We feel the refusal of real grief in all the differing forms of emotional immobility that afflict us and that actually take enormous effort to maintain (which is why the refusal to feel is so exhausting). Unhappiness faithfully followed leads us to the place where we are keeping back all the tears: tears or even a need for helpless weeping where helpless weeping might be the only way to reach the ground that underlies our very refusal to come to ground.

In the end, when our discontent and our interior grief is fully felt, our surface sadness falls away and opens the door to desire again: we allow ourselves to want again what I have not allowed myself to want; to deserve what I did not feel I ever deserved. Unhappiness fully felt, can get me out of the house and on the road again; even if I have to travel through further forms of difficulty and discontent. Setting off sincerely on this pilgrim journey I am now on my way to a place so intriguing that the journey itself always makes sense of any brief visitations of discontent.

Unhappiness is a state that gifts us an extraordinary self-compassion: simply by its own definition, unhappiness tells us there is someone else I want to be, someone else I want to travel with and somewhere over the horizon I want to eventually find: and that all those invitations live continually in my mind and body in a way that must be answered, whether I wish them to invite me or not.

Finally, unhappiness and discontent followed to their source, eliminate boredom in a human life: they lead unerringly to difficulty and drama, in fact our lives might be too tedious to endure without the discontent that fuels our spectacular dramas and the unending, entertaining melodramas of others, all spurred on by various forms of unhappiness. If our sincere pilgrimage through those dramas leads to a deeper, more grounded, more generous arrival in this life, then all our dramas become stories worth telling again to others.

Unhappiness always becomes, in the end, the story of how we got here, to this better place. Sometimes everything has to be inscribed dramatically across the heavens, so we can find that one line, already written inside us, and written at a deeper level than we could ever know.

carries two, beautiful, resonant almost underground vowel sounds echoing through its very centre, as if the word itself brings more meaning than our bodies or our minds are able to hold or understand. Said fully and properly the word unknown sets the whole thoracic region resonating in turn, in the same way the unknown itself resonates through every minute structure of our never fully-articulated life. Unknown is a word that always echoes, spoken or unspoken, through the hidden structures of our barely articulated lives.

Every known in our life, almost by definition, communicates with, lives with and grows with, not only the invitational mystery of its own accompanying and as yet, unknown future, but with the way our present understanding of what we know will be rearranged by what we will come to know. What we know and describe now, will be seen and known and described in a radically different way by our future self, and most especially by that future self, granted the perspective of our deathbed and preparing itself for the greatest unknown of all.

Most human beings find themselves, at times, longing for a settled existence and yet any settled existence without the unknown to draw it on and enliven it eventually becomes a prison from which we become more than desperate to escape. We often think of a committed relationship as a way of eliminating too much of the unknown in our lives, a way of settling down, and yet our intimate relationships are prime examples of the way the known and the unknown live together, and in the very same way we try to live together, in a kitchen, in a bedroom or in a car traveling together, speaking of the things we know and do not know while facing toward the unknown future to which we are traveling.

Every beginning to get to know, in every relationship, is also a never-ending getting to know, a tidal exchange between what we can comprehend and understand and what breathes a surprising and alternative life into our mutual understanding.

Strangely, what draws us initially into thinking we can anchor our life in one known committed life, is the seduction inherent in all the ways the other represents so much of the unknown. What is most seductive in that intimate other to which we are first attracted is the rich cargo of the unknown that by slowly getting to know them, bumps, floats and eddies into our life carried not only by their unspoken past but their slowly understood hopes and dreams for the future. What is then beguiling in a solemn commitment to that same person is sharing all our present delightful knowns with all the unknowns we share together. What enlivens every relationship and continues to enliven it is the invitation to the edge between what can now be said and what is waiting to be said, out of the shared unknown.

No matter the settled nature of any individual life, the unknown accompanies us through every turn of our attempt to know a person, a work or an epoch of our life more thoroughly. The person we might have named and boxed and predicted a future for, the person we think we know so well in a marriage, or a settled relationship, that colleague whom we have assessed with too small a name, all the while as we continue to name them, becoming something of a stranger to us, becoming a stranger even to themselves, someone they themselves have to get to know again; someone therefore, we in turn have to meet and get to know again. All knowns live in a marriage or a friendship with their own seemingly faithful, accompanying and emerging, unknowns. The presence of the unknown is always the arbiter of health in any relationship, the willingness to join the conversation between the hidden essence of a person and the as yet unspoken future to which they are drawn.

Even the most cherished memories of things that happened in our life or of people who occupied our past so poignantly begin to change as our own maturing sense of self starts to enter ground it has never explored before, and from that ground, see things we never saw before. In the light of that seeing, what we heard and witnessed, and what we now remember begins to change into something surprising. The person we condemned as our enemy in divorce, we realise now was just a fellow struggler, like ourselves, trying to emerge with some shred of dignity intact: the annoying competitor in our field, now seen as the one who enlivened our own dedication and pushed us into creative territory we might never have entered without them.

What we see and know as settled fact in our life right now is already growing and changing into something else. We get to know and get to love not only the things we cherish, but all the ways we have learned to protect ourselves from vulnerabilities that loving in an even deeper way entails. We love the things we love, but we also learn too quickly to love the things that prevent us undergoing the heartache of living and loving in a deeper, more open, more generous way.

For all that we say again and again, that we are afraid of the unknown, we are actually not afraid of the unknown, what we might be more afraid of, is letting go of what we know so well, and have learned, with so much difficulty, to love so well, until now.

UNORDINARY

is a word that belongs to our future, a word that could open up a different understanding of what it means to be singular, what it means to be communally human, and above all, what it means to be here, in this difficult world; all of us, every one of us, trying to live an extraordinary, ordinary life.

Unordinary might be a more merciful word than the word extraordinary. Extraordinary is too extraordinary a word. We often wield the word extraordinary as a weapon against ourselves: wanting to be extraordinary has us thinking we need to be another, better version of ourselves: a virtuoso violinist, a genius mathematician, a luminary in the field of literature. Extraordinary is a word that has us emulating what others carry easily in themselves but that for us, emulating another, almost always becomes a burden: extraordinary is what I would like to be, unordinary is what I am already, hidden inside me, but which is waiting to be revealed, under the guise of my ordinary life.

Unordinary carries a sense of uncovering, of finding something undefinable but precious beneath the surface of the world, beneath the surface of my everyday self and my everyday life. The words beneath the words, the gift at the centre of what is offered at the surface. Extraordinary is almost always approached through doing, unordinary is approached and uncovered through undoing, through a radical simplification of what I know about myself and my world.

All artistic paths and almost all paths of self-knowledge begin with inspiration from and emulation of another's extraordinary gifts: an astonishing musical performance fully heard, a masterly painting seen, dancers witnessed in awe - in our witness is the gift of their easy un-ordinariness, brought out as sheer unassailable presence. Admiration and emulation is always where we start in attempting the extraordinary but all paths of emulation taken too far become paths of impersonation: I am not that person no matter how much I sound like them, in my voice, on the violin, in the meeting room, on the dance floor. My unordinary self is so much more difficult to approach than my extraordinary self.

Extraordinary is something we might want to become or could become; unordinary is what lies beneath my everyday life, like an interior seam of precious metal hidden by layers of my surface ordinariness; something to be uncovered and perhaps at times, even unleashed. Unordinary says there is something yet to be seen in me, something yet to emerge. Unordinary is the ordinary me, but half-a-shade braver than my surface-self because it has to be brought out from what is hidden. The extraordinary might take effort and constant practice, but bringing out the unordinary from the hidden takes real, personal courage.

The extraordinary is what others witness in me when I go through the full measure of undoing and uncovering that reveals my unordinary, ordinary self. The ease of the bow across the strings creating the sublime, the easy aplomb with which I orchestrate a meeting, the deft touch of the potter's hand against the wet, spinning clay. Unordinary is the ultimate experience of absolute presence, complete personal expression and a burgeoning sense of freedom amidst all our responsibilities and our many duties.

Unordinary is worthy of a lifetime's dedication and a lifetime's journey; and yet, in such an extraordinary way, unordinary is always, always, always, just a single step away from my ordinary, everyday life.

VANITY

is the first step toward religious revelation. In the illusory awareness of our own overwhelming youthful beauty, we have the first intuitions of being seen by something other than, and greater than, ourselves. In the first innocent sense of how astonishingly impressive we are, or how intelligent we might be, no matter how fatuous, how misplaced or even how hilarious our self-appointed perspective, we have the primary and foundational intuition of an essential individuality: we have the first understanding of an astonishing underlying uniqueness. Vanity is the timeless underlying revelation of having been seen and being found by the world. Vanity tells me, to my initial cost but to my eventual favour, that I have not only been seen to have been given a gift but that I am myself, a gift.

The mystery that always lies behind our particular, individual form of vanity lies in the constant daily invitation to understand what kind of gift we actually have underneath that surface preoccupation; what might be seen in us under our self delusion, and what gift we are seen to give. Our gift is almost always in a state where it has yet to be truly determined and there lies our path and our pilgrimage through the trials of seeing and being seen. We fall in love with our outer complexion in the mirror, seeing through our own appreciative eyes the eyes of others seeing us. Vanity may be admiration of our own, highly polished shoes but it also allows us, gradually, step by step, and humiliation by humiliation, to stand in other people's shoes; the shoes of people who carry the same surface illusions as we do.

The surface illusions of vanity we share with everyone carry their own pleasures and their own joys, most especially when we are young. Youthful vanities, can also be, when the stars align, a true reflection of an inner state - moments where we are seen and seen in our best light - can be deeply satisfying in the way they marry what is inside me with what is outside me: the perfect dress, like a new blossom itself when worn by blossoming peach-like youth, a moment on stage singing our heart out in the spotlight, the perfect jacket worn at the perfect age; many times, the right word said at the right time impressing the surrounding crowd, representing something both helpful and truthful, the sometimes obvious vanity of the speaker subordinate to the truth of what has been said, all, all, sudden revelations of what was previously hidden inside, revealing a person suddenly seen by the world.

Vanity is always its own cure and always leads us to our maturity through the difficult but inevitable doorway of humiliation. The first self-regarding stage of vanity is always brought to an end by vanity itself. Walking quickly past a lifetime of mirrors, catching glimpses of our selves as we go, we are always surprised to find ourselves suddenly humiliated rather than venerated through other's eyes, our stance against the light now revealing our belly rather than our profile, our old style outline amusing the sceptical young who smile back condescendingly at our old-fashioned antics: more embarrassingly, we have the familiar rip in the pants, seen by others, but not by ourselves. No it is all, all just a matter of time before we find ourselves being found out: that moment in our late forties where we suddenly realise that people are not seeing someone in their early thirties: the pulling in of our belly that tells others not that we are slim but that we are just pulling in our belly. We are first horrified, shamed a little and then invited to catch up with ourselves; to admit to the actual ground on which we stand and the threshold through which we are now passing. Vanity asks me to continue to love myself through the continual humiliating arrivals and a coming to ground in the humility that maturation involves. Each humiliating step of self-discovery precipitated by my vanity is a step toward self knowledge and self-understanding.

Luckily, from the point of view of personal growth, any increase in our vanity only ripens us for greater public humiliation and therefore a more instructive and forceful learning. Vanity is self-correcting in the merciful devastation of self-discovery. We are all, in fact, unconsciously waiting to be embarrassed into the next dispensation of our existence and the next clear territory of our understanding. Perhaps, if we were quicker learners, we might just, in the moment of absolute public humiliation, say a very loud 'thank you' to everyone concerned for being undeceived in such a clear, public and instructive way, instead of our usual recourse: turning bright red, shuffling off the scene and retreating in obvious embarrassment.

We can all comfort ourselves that vanity might be one of the last cloaks we throw off before we die, spiritually or physically - even Zen monks look rather sharp in their black vestments - the handsome bells, the polished floors, the shaved head another kind of self proclamation, saying look at us and the mighty commitment we have made! No, enlightened or unenlightened we were all made to be looked at, and the world itself was made to look itself in the mirror, which is why we find them everywhere we go. There are other mirrors surrounding us too: the reflective, miraculous power of those elemental constellating glories we call the natural world. What would the glory of a flower be if it could not be seen or admired by the birds, the bees and even the busy? We are all, every one of us, born to be seen and admired. From our first winning, cooing appearance as a baby, we were made ripe for the path of vanity and corrective humiliation, and we can all be comforted by the fact that, what we want others to see in us, and the depth to which we wish them to see it, changes inexorably toward the real, the authentic, and necessary, the closer we get to no longer being seen at all.

YOU

is not just you: *you* is a word that reveals *me* in remarkable ways by the very emphasis in the way I use you.

You is a small word that has a very large influence on the way I reveal myself: you is an extraordinary indicator and a calibration of our relationship with everything and everyone to which we give that label.

You is an ambitious word considering I hardly know you at all. *You* is a word I use to try and embrace all the players in my drama, as if I know the ultimate parts they play. *You* is the one I only think I know and the one always just beyond my grasp.

You is the word I use without a thought, a hundred times a day, never able to fully acknowledge its immense power: the way it can carry an intimate invitation to others to enter fully into the centre of my life; send them away into the distance or more usually to freeze them in limbo, keeping them tactically in confusion, caught between the warmth of welcome and the coldness of distance. *You* can be the *thou* of closeness or the *you* of accusation and in an extraordinary way, in virtuoso hands, every single gradation in between. How I say the word *you* calibrates my intimacy or distance from *you*, or from the world, but also in the way I address myself, how distant I might be from my own body and from the live conversation between what I think is me and what I have decided and named as *you*. *You* is both my door of hospitality and my barrier to keep out the world.

You closes the gap between me and the world to a warm, flowing intimacy or extends it a thousand miles over a cold and distant horizon. *You* will do for almost everything. You is constantly in my mouth for everything and everybody: both in my assessments of everyone and everybody and in my relationship with everything and everybody. *You* occupies the whole three dimensional, three hundred and sixty degree spectrum of a world that seems to both surround me and dwell beyond the range of my understanding.

You is also used to go beneath the horizon of my own inner understanding. I will often talk to myself, addressing the inner me as *you*, and that *you* is often accompanied by my own name, in exhortation, in accusation and sometimes, after sinning, even in shame.

You is my attempt to name something I cannot really name and so often the way I say *you* is often an emblem of my powerlessness. The way I say *you* in accusation, in invitation or in guarded neutrality signals and advertises in an intimately revealing form, all of my ultimate psychological vulnerabilities, all the ways I wish to invite the world through my door and all the ways I wish to keep it safely at bay.

You is the constant calibration of my ability for intimacy spoken a hundred times a day. *You*, when said to *me*, echoes right through me to another me, undergirding my understanding. *You* is always how, in my relationships, in my work, in my attempted encouragement and criticisms of others, I find a generous, if unconscious way of telling *you* as much as I can, about *me*.

ZEN

is a great, big, magnificent, all-embracing seduction of a word. Zen is a beguiling and charming philanderer of the first order, that good looking stranger who lets us fall in love, and then runs off with someone else, so that we can fall out of love with the word and be let alone in our grief, to fall in love with reality.

Zen is a centuries old, glamorous, disguised, cover-up: inviting us in, in each succeeding generation, so exquisitely, so quietly, so subtly, so seductively into its grip, that we do not, to begin with, have any understanding of what we have become, so innocently, ensnared by; we do not have a clue as to the way we are being taken in so swiftly and so unerringly into the currents that lead to the edge of our own necessary, physical and emotional breakdown. Amidst our hopes for polished wood, serene surroundings, the sound of bells and the whispered shuffle of bare feet, we always find, to our consternation, that Zen always begins and ends in tears.

The first tears in Zen practice are for our bodies and our restless minds: for our backs, our knees and for our legs, trying to sit upright on those strangely necessary black cushions. The next tears are for our hearts, our emotions and our previously imprisoned minds. The last tears are for a joy and laughter that still, to our amazement, keeps a friendship and an understanding with our previous griefs. Zen is the journey we take through heartbreak. At the last heartbreak, Zen retires from the field, Zen generously disappears and lets us alone, refusing to let us use the word so freely again, refusing to let us be fooled by what we originally needed to be so enticed by.

Drawn toward Zen practice, we almost always fall in love with the word itself. Zen beguiles us with that barely breathing vowel sound that lives so eternally and so glamorously at its centre, between the dashing capital Z and that oh-so subtle brushstroke of an 'n'. The word itself seems to be clean and rested, insightful and eternally hip, something inspiring: something that conjures light and space, and a welcome order amidst a difficult world of besiegement, chaos and successive, never-ending experiences of grief.

We fall for the word as we fall for the deep silences that swim dreamily through the first pains of our practice, Zen welcomes us through its invitation to a sense of spacious ease, to freedom from worry and thankfully in our mind's eye, to a deeper form of rested presence - a presence we first saw in the clean, perfectly proportioned spaces inherited so seductively from Japan - but then, as Zen breaks down the divisions in our mind and body, we find our sense of self breaks down too, firstly from the inside out and then, at the end, from the outside in. We learn to bow in the Zendo, not knowing what we are rehearsing: unconsciously preparing as we are, to duck through the achingly low doors of abasement our heartbreak will provide.

We pass through those low doors as we pass into the difficulties of marriage or intimate relationship. Like the raw vulnerabilities we find in the commitments of marriage or in a long, intimate partnership, Zen begins with the honeymoon of getting to know, graduates through difficult and unwanted surprises and then culminates in a slow breakdown, day by day, through the trials and invitations of intimacy and heartache itself.

As in a marriage, in Zen we learn that the line between this body, another's body and the body of the world, is not where we thought it was. As in a love relationship, we learn that what we thought we knew is not equal to what we are discovering. As in an intimate relationship, we learn that who we thought we were is not who we are now in the midst of all the disappearing boundaries. Almost always in relationship, what we think we have to give is not what is needed; what we thought was love might not have been love at all, and what we thought we had to give up is not, after all, what is being asked for.

Tellingly, as in relationship, the hardest thing to do in Zen practice is simply finding a way to breath freely while staying connected to the world, or the world of another. Breathing is foundational to both coming to know and letting go of what we think we know. Like the things we think we know about relationship, all the things we thought we knew about Zen will have to be given up at the end and even then, Zen and the intimacies of relationship both ask us to give up the very last thing, the very thing for which we thought we had already given everything up. Like the essence of intimate relationship, the very essence of Zen might be giving up and giving in, not to our partner but to what the essence and heartache of the partnership calls us to.

Zen is surprising under its subterfuge: Zen's biggest surprise is that it seems to have more confidence in the incoherent life we first brought to it than the one we are trying to replace it with. We find ourselves seen at the core as one who generated difficulties not because our essence is difficulty but because difficulties were what we thought we needed: in order to get through; in order to be worthy of something better, difficulty was our needed friend, difficult is how we thought things should be. Difficult is what we thought we were.

In the attempt to give our old life away and have it replaced by the newly spacious clarity we first glimpse in Zen, we find it constantly returned to us, in a voice that says we will never need anything more than what we already had. We are told in no uncertain terms that we were more miraculous in our simple wish to find a way than any abstracted spacious place we could reach through sitting in silence. And yet, sitting in silence is how we will find this out.

Zen frustrates us, wants us to find the way just by being the very essence of things that find their way. Zen, in the old cliché, because it is so true, wants us to be the way itself. It might be that Zen as a word would like us to understand this one simple thing so it can to go home and have a good rest. Zen begins by being the hand seemingly raised to keep us at bay and then slowly and imperceptibly is seen to be the hand that rests on our shoulder, telling us we might be fine, just as we are. When we actually glimpse what we are: we and that hand seem to disappear altogether, simply because there is no need for a hand when the reluctant body that needed it has disappeared.

Zen is indeed, an old fraudster, but one with a heart of gold. Just as we are taken in, it relents and to our relief, gives us our money back. Zen, we realise in the end, is much humbler in its aims than we thought it was, Zen we realise is more realistic than we thought it was, Zen in the end, is always surprisingly practical, and helpful, and just wants us to do the simplest, most obvious thing. Zen doesn't waste its energy by choosing too early in the game and waits for things to make their own choice unimpeded by interference. Zen refuses to choose between light and dark, restlessness and order; between not knowing or having answers. Zen has a well-cultivated sense of humour and carries its own hidden cargo of amusement at all our self-deceptions and false choices, Zen is a true comedian at times, its most hilarious proposition being that you might not, after all, have to believe in your own thoughts.

We walk toward Zen as if toward a door of light but Zen practice moves us just as much and unerringly toward a door into the dark, into what until now we could not see or discern, so that we might better understand what we might have hidden there, but also so that we might better understand the underlying miracle of light itself.

Zen leads us on like the very best kind of guide, as if we are equal to what we will eventually find. Zen is the ultimate kind of guide, in that it disappears in the moment of our understanding, to leave us with what we have found, and more importantly and to our astonishment, what comes to find us.

If Zen asks us to begin with, to follow the thread of heartbreak: then to begin with, heartbreak is the only thread we need to follow. Heartbreak has many difficult doors, almost all of them leading where we hoped and prayed we did not need to go.

Reading between the lines, the old Zen teachers seemed to think that one heartbreak is as good as another - so many doors! All heartbreak is giving up: but the mercy that lies in the path of heartbreak is that, in the end, we will have to give up even our precious, well-guarded memories of heartbreak itself.

In real heartbreak something else always comes to find us. On the other side of heartbreak there is an experience of timeless radiance that cannot be described from this side of heartbreak: so for now, sitting Zen, and carrying the silence from sitting into our lives, heartbreak is all we need to know.

Our breath in true heartbreak is faithful to the literal ease or the stress in our physical heart, and in following the path to heartbreak faithfully - whether we are black-clad Zen students facing a wall, or broken down unrequited lovers facing being left - in the raw grief of feeling abandoned, the breath becomes deeply even, spacious and self-healing. Weeping wholeheartedly is a rare experience in a human life exactly because weeping wholeheartedly to the point of breakdown might be the only experience of enlightenment most human beings experience.

Zen is a word that asks us to do nothing more than what it has to do so generously itself: get over itself, get tired of itself and in the end get rid of itself. Zen is a word that generously arranges for its own disappearance just as we ourselves have to arrange for our own going. Zen leaves us in the end saying we might be just as much alive and just as much deserving and just as much enlightened in the midst of the mess we brought to it as we are now, under its beguiling influence, with our straight backs, our fully remembered sutras and our perfect breathing.

No, what you wanted from the word, you already had, you had just forgotten, and it was the forgetting itself that was most painful, more than what you thought was the pain itself, so you came this way as the only way you could, by allowing yourself to be fooled, as we often do, by a great romance, by a great long drama of a journey, by that beautiful, beguiling temptress of a word, Zen, so that it could unerringly and kindly lead you back to the door of heartbreak again, so that you could enter it fully this time, so that your grief this time could be let alone to be its own beautiful self and its own beautiful cure, so that you could find yourself as you wanted, just waiting in the full vulnerability of waiting, or breathing, as you always somehow knew it was possible to breathe, in the full amplitude of breathing, so that you could enter at last the hallway of love, and then in turn, beyond that, be entered by the place you thought it was never possible to reach.